The Cincinnati Cookbook

THE IOWA
SZATHMÁRY
CULINARY ARTS SERIES

Edited by David E. Schoonover

THE
Cincinnati Cookbook

Household Guide
Embracing Menu, Daily Recipes,
Doctors Prescriptions and
Various Suggestions for the
Coming Generation

EDITED BY

David E. Schoonover

University of Iowa Press   ᗐ   Iowa City

University of Iowa Press, Iowa City 52242

Foreword copyright © 1994 by the

University of Iowa Press

Printed in the United States of America

Originally published in 1908 by the F. C. H. Manns
Company, Cincinnati, Ohio

Printed on acid-free paper

Library of Congress Cataloging-in-Publication Data
The Cincinnati cookbook: household guide embracing
menu, daily recipes, doctors prescriptions and various
suggestions for the coming generation / edited by
David E. Schoonover.

     p.   cm.—(The Iowa Szathmáry culinary arts
series)

   "Originally published in 1908 by the F. C. H. Manns
Company, Cincinnati, Ohio"—T.p. verso.

   Includes index.

   ISBN 0-87745-460-4 (alk. paper)

   1. Cookery, American.   2. Home economics.
3. Cincinnati (Ohio)—History.   I. Schoonover, David E.
II. Series.

TX715.C5742   1994

641.5973—dc20   93-23630

                                       CIP

01 00 99 98 97 96 95 94   C   5 4 3 2 1

Foreword

David E. Schoonover

For the fifth volume in the Iowa Szathmáry Culinary Arts Series we have chosen to return to the Midwest. The all-encompassing *Cincinnati Cookbook: Household Guide Embracing Menu, Daily Recipes, Doctors Prescriptions and Various Suggestions for the Coming Genera-ion,* first published in 1908, is illustrated with intriguing turn-of-the-century ads facing almost every recipe page. The guide also includes photographs of the Cincinnati area, its buildings, and its prominent community benefactors.

CULINARY FEATURES

The Cincinnati Cookbook opens with "Information for the Beginners," containing suggestions for managing "the countless little essentials to the perfect home." The "Beginners" receive special advice about "Dinner Giving": "So much can be said on this subject, as the well-being of humanity is essentially connected with the perfection of the cuisine."

Despite the book's stated intentions to offer helpful advice, it is sometimes difficult to discern the rationale of its organization. The first twenty-two pages contain recipes for breads, cookies, cakes, and icings, then salads and salad dressings, followed by oysters, crabs, sardines, and veal loaf. Next come Spanish cream, cream salmon, then cream puffs, presumably having cream in common, followed by potato puffs. After soups, pickles, and more dressings and salads comes a page of household hints, with a preparation for cleaning carpets and kid gloves and a warning about washing your face in ordinary lake water. The text from pages 65 to 241 is devoted to food items. The guide concludes with "Household Hints" for remedying coughs, toothaches, earaches, croup, fainting, and sunstroke. A list of "Medicinal Food" explains their various efficacies.

Finally, "Miscellaneous Recipes" explain how to deal with insects, laundry, and other cleaning chores (see especially "To Clean Black Dress Silks").

Unlike the first volume in the series, *P.E.O. Cook Book: Souvenir Edition*, which calls for "butter size of egg" for Creamed Shrimps or "alum size of walnut" for Cucumber Mangoes, *The Cincinnati Cookbook* uses accurate measures and weights throughout.

The Cincinnati Cookbook prescribes cooking temperatures as "slow oven," "rather cool oven," "moderate oven," "hot oven," "rather a quick oven," "steady, but not quick, oven," and "quick oven." The directions for Angel Cake call for placing it "carefully in an oven of moderate temperature. . . . Success depends largely upon having the oven the proper temperature; if too warm, the cake will be tough."

COMMERCIAL WISDOM

The Cincinnati Cookbook was first published as a commercial enterprise on a large scale, underwritten by seventy-two advertisers and prepared "for the new housewife given to you gratis." Not surprisingly, *The Cincinnati Cookbook* contains a strong element of boosterism, starting with its publisher's motto, "Opportunities Come to All Men Who Hustle" (quoted three different places in the book). On an equally positive note, one advertiser urges readers to "Start right when you begin housekeeping. Be sure that you get started right. The rest will then be easy."

The advertisers give a full taste of the advice that Sinclair Lewis would vigorously lampoon later in *Babbitt* and *Main Street*. Some wisdom is financial: "Start now to get a home of your own, because success or failure in life depends upon grasping opportunities. . . ." Another advertiser gives positive encouragement to the new housewife: "To satisfy your husband buy and use Banner Bread (at your grocer)—then you will be happy." Others warn of things that can spoil: "Tainted butter and milk that is not quite fresh do not enhance domestic bliss." Aunt Molly skillfully combines positive and negative aspects of homemaking: "It is an easy matter for the bride who is a good cook to retain the love of her husband. A man who is poorly, or improperly fed, soon loses his health, and becomes cross and dissatisfied."

"VARIOUS SUGGESTIONS FOR THE COMING GENERATION"

The Cincinnati Cookbook's introductory "Information for the Beginners" concludes with "How To Please Husbands," a recipe for selecting, preserving, comforting, warming, and spicing the husband-in-hand. Two other culinary booklets in the Szathmáry Collection attribute this same advice to "One of the lecturers before the Baltimore Cooking School." Still other versions differing slightly in titles and wording were served up for more than thirty years. In a quick survey of midwestern pamphlets, I discovered "A Recipe for Cooking Husbands," then "How to Cook a Husband," and finally "How to Preserve Husbands."

Near the middle of the guide appears another recipe, offering "Directions for Making a Charming Young Lady." A curious reader may wonder why such information is located on page 151 between Soft Soap and Early Sleep, following recipes on page 149 for Hominy and Toast. These helpful hints provide an enlightening glimpse into the process of gender-specific socialization disguised as humor. The suggestions may strike present-day readers as cute and quaint, arch and cloying, or egregiously sexist and offensive, yet they are truly recipes for their time.

BENEFACTORS AND CINCINNATI'S CIVIC HISTORY

The Cincinnati Cookbook includes not only photographs of a number of the city's geographical areas, buildings, schools, and monuments but also portraits of several generous and important donors to the city's cultural institutions. Their contributions are not identified in the book, perhaps because their benefactions were so well known as not to need explanation. Several historical books on Cincinnati contain multiple references to these leading citizens.

Ruben R. Springer (p. 56) in May 1875 offered to give $125,000 for a music hall if an equal sum could be raised by the citizens. The hall cost much more, and Springer eventually contributed $235,000. He made other gifts to the exposition building, the Odeon, and helped endow the College of Music of Cincinnati.

In 1892 J. G. Schmidlapp (p. 72) established a concert fund of $50,000, the income from which was used to pay the bands for Sunday music at the Art Academy's bandstand. Schmidlapp later gave an annex to the Fine Arts Museum in remembrance of his wife. He was also responsible for the Schmidlapp Apartments, built in 1911 to prove that good housing at low cost could be made available to the poor.

Henry Probasco (p. 104) donated the Tyler-Davidson Fountain, completed in 1871–72, to honor his deceased business partner and brother-in-law, Tyler Davidson. It depicts the blessings of water, featuring the "genius of Water," and shows water quenching fires and thirst.

Mrs. Frederick H. Alms (p. 202) gave a wing to the Fine Arts Museum and gave Alms Park in 1916 as a memorial to her husband.

HISTORY AND NEWS

To gain some sense of the flavors of Cincinnati in the year the guide first appeared, I reviewed issues of the *Cincinnati Enquirer* for 1907–1908. Some of the year's "Fashionable Arrangements" included a performance by the Harvard Glee Club at the Odeon, a debutante riding class, a musical ride and dance at the Riding Club, and a dinner in honor of the Yale Glee Club. The "Younger Set" had dances, card parties, a cotillion, a mask and domino party, and a theater party. Appropriately for the snowy season, the Country Club held a "Bal de Neige" in December as part of the year's debuts.

Several of Cincinnati's natives and prominent citizens gathered with President-Elect Taft to celebrate Thanksgiving. Melville E. Ingalls, former president of the Big Four Railroad, hosted the stag dinner at his cabin. J. G. Schmidlapp, capitalist and one of the guide's benefactors, attended as one of Taft's longtime friends.

In January the great Polish pianist and composer Ignacy Jan Paderewski presented a concert at the Music Hall. In the same month, the Cincinnati Art Club sponsored an evening lecture by F. Hopkinson Smith, author of *Caleb West, Master Diver* and a prolific and popular novelist, illustrator, and essayist.

The theater scene included "The Lion and the Mouse," "The Parisian Model," and a pair of western entertainments, "Texas, A Romance of the Southern Plains" and "Sheriff of Angel Gulch."

Those in a hurry could enjoy Dickens's *Oliver Twist*, Schiller's *William Tell*, and Goethe's *Faust* as "A Classic in a Page," while those with more time could be thrilled with *The Trail of the Lonesome Pine* by John Fox, Jr.—"It is easy to see why this story started off with an edition of 100,000 copies. There are no dull chapters between its covers."

Readers learned of the "Wonderful Power of the Pie. The mysterious pastry has played a part in love, war, and religion." Economy-minded seafood shoppers, even in Cincinnati, could order a whale steak for 10 cents and had these choices in oysters: fried oysters, oyster fritters, oysters and sweetbreads, poor man's oysters, creamed oysters, oyster patties, oyster cutlets, and oyster sauce.

Feature writers also promoted thriftiness through poetry:

"How to Prevent Waste in the Kitchen"

Wicked waste makes woeful want,
and you may live to say,

"Oh, that I had that piece of bread
which I once threw away"

The *Enquirer* also recounted several extraordinary food-related tidbits:

LOAF of bread
Riz Right Up From Plate on the Table and Then Fell,
Terrifying the Witnesses

Dinner Is Served in Her Auto And Other Eccentricities
Indulged in by Mrs. Patterson—Victim of Heiress Hunter

Moonshiners More Trouble As Temperance Wave Sweeps South

As an example of what it might cost to purchase food items, in 1907 Kroger Grocery and Baking Company had eighty-three stores offering foods at the following prices: loin steaks, 12½¢ a pound; fresh hams, 10¢ a pound; smoked hams, 12¢ a pound; grits, 2 pounds for 5¢; "Vinegar-Pickled Pigs Feet," a 200-pound barrel for $8.25; Alaska salmon, 12¢ a can; "Dessert Brand of Extra Standard Lemon Cling California Peaches," 25¢; and "Detrick's Real Old Whiskey at 4 Full Quarts," $3.20.

The cook could acquire a new Spear's "Good Will Art Range" for $25.00, guaranteed for twenty years; terms: $1.00 cash, 50¢ a week.

Cincinnati's hotels offered a variety of options, from the "New Beautiful Hotel Savoy—Rooms $1.00—Up," including free showers or tub baths, telephone service, and hot or cold running water, to the Hotel Havlin, whose "Grill Room Special" luncheon cost 50 Cents, with the "Special Table d'Hote Dinner" costing $1.00.

Advertisers offered consumers a marvelous range of products: "Test for Yourself the Wonderful Curative Properties of Swamp-Root." "A Health Visitor comes into thousands of homes every morning, bringing rosy health, steady nerves and a clear brain—POSTUM." "The Wiedemann Beers bring to the mother of children the healthy, wholesome beauty of a happy woman." "Pure Food. No Food Commissioner of any State has ever attacked the absolute purity of Grape-Nuts."

Cincinnati has long been known for its geographical, economic, political, cultural, and culinary diversity. *The Cincinnati Cookbook*, through its recipes, advice, and advertisements, illuminates many of these qualities of the Queen City.

THE IOWA SZATHMÁRY CULINARY ARTS SERIES

Many readers and collectors of cookbooks now agree with the *New York Times* that "Prose, Not Recipes, Sells Today's Food Books" (May 15, 1991) and that "The History of Food [Has Gained] a Scholarly Pedigree" (May 30, 1984).

The cookbooks appearing in our series are selected from the Szathmáry Collection of Culinary Arts, comprising more than 8,000 volumes, representing more than 500 years of books and manuscripts on all aspects of food and its history. The series provides today's readers and collectors with much more than recipes. Many of these cookbooks, such as *The Cincinnati Cookbook*, contain introductions, perhaps literary or historical matter, period advertisements, or a variety of illustrations that are interesting in themselves. The cultural context of cookbooks is also important—who published them, for what audience, in what time period?

The series began with two books having midwestern origins. In spring 1992 the *P.E.O. Cook Book: Souvenir Edition*, chosen for its Iowa and midwestern connections, was reprinted in facsimile from the 1908 edition published in Knoxville, Iowa. We believed that readers would be interested not only in its 575 recipes but also in the twenty-five black-and-white photographs of public buildings and private residences in Knoxville.

The second volume, also published in spring 1992, was Nelson Algren's *America Eats*, a previously unpublished manuscript containing Algren's research into midwestern food and foodways, illustrated with photographs from the State Historical Society of Iowa.

For the third volume, published in fall 1992, we selected a more exotic text, *The Khwan Niamut: or, Nawab's Domestic Cookery*, a rare collection of Persian recipes translated into English and printed in Calcutta in 1839.

The fourth volume, issued in spring 1993, was Edward Kidder's *Receipts of Pastry & Cookery: For the Use of His Scholars*, an undated manuscript probably prepared in the 1740s, which was reproduced in facsimile, accompanied by a transcription, with additional recipes from Kidder's contemporaries and a glossary.

Future volumes already in preparation for the series include our first translation, *Kochbuch 1905 Käth. Schratt*, owned by the mistress of Emperor Franz Joseph of Austria, king of Hungary. The book itself, written by hand, is a fascinating collection of French, Austrian, Hungarian, Bohemian, and other recipes. Later we will be publishing the earliest English cookery compilation in our archive, *The Receiptes Booke of Robert Godfrey* (1665), which belonged first to Lady Borlase of Bockmore Manor.

ACKNOWLEDGMENTS

I would like to express my appreciation to these colleagues at the University of Iowa Libraries for their encouragement and assistance with this project: Sheila Creth, Edward Shreeves, Robert McCown, and Susan Hansen.

The Cincinnati Cookbook

"OPPORTUNITIES COME TO ALL MEN WHO HUSTLE"—MANNS.

OUR   MOTTO

THE F. C. H. MANNS CO.
PRINTERS & ENGRAVERS
CINCINNATI, OHIO.

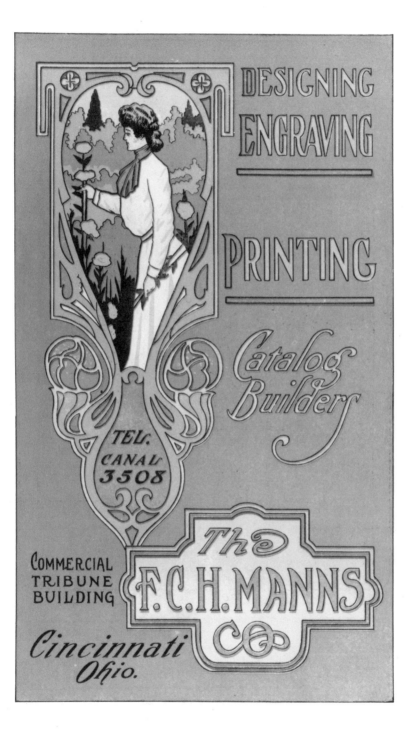

Information for the Beginners.

It has always been a question of making home-life replete with happiness and comfort which is so dear to the busy wife. She it is who thinks of the countless little essentials to the perfect home, and smooths over the little worries with a persistent cheerfulness that makes life brighter and better for the giving. Men very often reproach the wife for a want of system in ordering our daily lives, but a careful woman will apportion her income to her expenditures with the utmost exactness, so much being set aside for each demand that is likely to be made upon it. A woman of this type loves to plan and contrive so that each object may have its fair share of the whole. Her House is well arranged because it is a reflection of her mind. There is a place for everything, and it does not ruffle her serenity to have things upset at times. She knows where they belong, and can easily put them back again. The perfect house-keeper will learn not only how to do everything, but also study and find the best and most simple methods of managing the whole.

It is a fact that many women regard the care of the home too much in the light of an incidental, permitting sundry little personal pleasures to rob their home of the necessary attention, leaving one at the close of each day with the unpleasant feeling of having accomplished nothing. This is not saying that women should confine themselves to the round of domestic employments, but the married woman who is willing to accept the home as her life-work will bring not only contentment and happiness to herself, but to others.

The order of the home, then is the first subject to be considered, and there should always be a sense of rest that confront and please the husband.

The making of a home is the most beautiful work that a woman can do, and it matters little whether her home be a small one in an isolated place, or a large one, in the midst of great activities. Each in her own place, reigning over her own kingdom, whether it is small or great, is either a noble success or a dismal failure. Within herself lies that which decides whether it shall be one or the other. This is a truth never to be lost sight of. It is an abundance of love in a household, or the lack of it there, which makes the difference between the family, where the daily meals are feeding times, more or less comfortable, and the one here they are the most delightful hours of the day.

The crowning grace of the home, in our opinion, is persistent cheerfulness and we should try to see the funny side of every annoyance. If any one is ill, we should discourage anxious inquiries after the health of the members of the family, believing that it is possible to talk yourself and others into any number of diseases.

The breakfast table should not be a bulletin-board for the curing of horrible dreams and depressing symptoms, but the place where a bright key-note for the day is struck. The supper table should not be made a battle-field, but a pleasing panorama of what has occurred during the day in the outer world.

The home need not be so immaculate in each minute and unseen part, but aim to make it a pleasant place to live in. Harmony is never monotonous. The mind of man is so susceptible to outward influences that he naturally falls into harmony with his surroundings, and takes upon himself the tone of thought and feeling that is suggested by them. If the room in which he lives or dines is unsuitably constructed, and ill-adapted for its intended use, it harasses and annoys him. Let each room in the home have its usefulness, and no matter how humble the surroundings, if neatness and cleanliness prevails, it cannot fail to bring happiness and contentment. Have a system about your most ordinary duties, and always bear in mind that to-day's privileges cannot be enjoyed, nor to-day's duties discharged to-morrow. To-morrow may never come. If it does come, it will bring its own privilege and duties—privilges made less, and duties made greater by to-day's neglect.

The young housekeeper must not become discouraged, but learn to "manage." Sit down quietly and plan your work. Do not try to copy your neighbor's houses nor their methods, but make your own little home just as you would have it, as far as you can. No good work was ever begun that obstacles and hindrances did not speedily present themselves, and the better the work, the more and greater do the difficulties often seem to be.

Every housekeeper should be a law unto herself in the ordering of the daily meals. Abolish routine and study surprises. Avoid the error of serving anyone dish (no matter how it is relished) until the family tires of it. Ingenuity and a little careful thought will work wonders. Life is made all the brighter by satisfactory feeding, and one is a dull philosopher, indeed, that despises a good dinner.

And last, but not least, let us say that the "good morning" should be the beginning of every day life. To say it pleasantly is to open the golden door of a day, and to make all the sunshine of life seem to rest upon you and reflect upon everybody else, and make them feel pleasant. One can work faster and easier when the heart is full of that liquid of love called pleasantness.

The successful wife does not win her laurels in merely perfecting herself in the culinary art, but in the careful study of the lives of others in her care, and how to promote their happiness in all the minor points of interest discussed in this chapter on the home. Ingenuity and love will surely show their beneficial results, in greater health and strength, and a consequent increase of happiness in living and in teaching others to live.

Now that we have made a little talk on the field of usefulness to the wives, it is our hope the thoughts suggested may sow seeds of happiness and contentment in the new home.

The Kitchen and Dining Room

The dining-room in every home should be as bright and sunny as possible. The plainest room can be made beautiful by exercising a little skill and good taste, and nothing contributes so much to one's happiness and appetite as pleasant surroundings.

The advisability of making dishes attractive by dainty serving is not enough appreciated by the busy housewife. It seems so much easier to dish the meat and vegetables "anyhow," than to use the extra exertion to make them pretty, that she is apt to grow careless. Habit is everything in such matters. The practice once acquired of arranging the food to please the eye, as well as the palate, the added labor is taken for granted and seldom observed. A bouquet of flowers, which may often be procured with little cost in the summer season, is better than a meal in some houses.

To add additional charm to your table, the following little observances may be mentioned: Garnish your stewed tomatoes and meat dishes with sprays of parsley, water-cress or celery tops, carrot tops, young beet leaves or lettuce, also make a pretty addition to many dishes. A dish of fruit is twice as tempting, if decorated with ferns, autumn leaves, or any graceful sprays of green. A little thought will easily indicate to the wife the simplest methods of serving various viands, and she will devise for herself dainty modes of garnishing and arranging dishes. Whatever tends to make food more appetizing in appearance will render it more so in reality. No one is quicker to notice the lack of grace and prettiness in one's surroundings than a man, only that he cannot tell so easily what is wanting. He is only conscious of a vague discomfort. In cookery recipes, we are almost tempted to add after each recipe, "Garnish this dish gracefully," or "serve tastefully," or "this dish should be served with quiet elegance, " etc.

Ease and simplicity should be the prevailing characteristics in every dining-room, avoiding any undue furnishing in the way of bric-a-brac, scarfs and drapery, which may add a charm to other rooms, but are sadly in the way in this apartment. Your dishes should shine, and show every evidence of careful washing, and your linen be snowy white and smoothly ironed.

The home dinner should be a most cheerful meeting of companionable and sprightly members, all interested in each other's welfare, all ready to contribute their quota to the general fund of enjoyment. The wife may be troubled about many things, but she should wear her pleasantest smiles at the table, that her husband may be refreshed in spirit as well as in body. The conversation should be bright and cheery.

Closely connected with the dining-room is the kitchen. The room in which all the fruit is prepared, all the cooking done and where all the pastry is gotten up should be of some importance. In this room, of all others, the old saying is most applicable, that "Cleanliness is next to Godliness." There is no reasonable excuse for thousands of disorderly and dirty kitchens all over the land. Water is plentiful and soap is cheap, and "Order is the first law of nature." Have a place for everything, and keep every thing in its place, and it will save you a multitude of steps, and enable you to do twice as much work in the same time. Money spent in the purchase of articles that will save labor time, is true economy; and if your kitchen is not supplied with everything necessary for convenient and successful housekeeping, begin at once to purchase, plan, arrange, and work, and your labors will soon be crowned with success. With proper management and a little taste everything can be kept in perfect order without over-taxing yourself.

In a well-ordered kitchen you will never find dirty pots, pans, skillets, dishes, or tinware. As soon as the meal is over, everything should be washed and put in its appropriate place. Let us give you a little insight into the science and management of your kitchen work. When you clear up your table, remove all the food first, then the sugar-bowl, butter-dish, etc. Then take a knife, and scrape all the crumbs from every plate and dish into the kitchen's pail, put all the bits of butter into the plate of cooking butter, and pour out all slops of tea, coffee, or water. Then pile up your dishes, placing the largest on the bottom, and so on, placing the pile in close proximity to the sink Mix in your dish-pan a quantity of warm water and a little soap. Wash each dish separately, beginning with glass and silver and ending with kettles and pans. After all are completed, wash out your dish-pan, and place as many of your dishes back in it, and rinse by pouring over them hot water, and dry rapidly. Follow this system daily, and you will be surprised at the rapidity with which you can accompilsh the regular routine of kitchen work. Everything will be done well, and your kitchen, which is indeed one of the most important rooms in the house, will always present an inviting appearance and you will have no occasion to feel any embarrassment should sudden visits be made to it by strangers.

In the chapter worth Knowing,'' many valuable hints will be given that will be of aid and benefit in the kitchen, and home in general, and they will be worthy of careful notice and adoption by the housewife.

Dinner Giving.

How many persons know how to give a dinner, set the table properly, and serve the foods in an orderly, appetizing way. So much can be said on this subject, as the well-being of humanity is essentially connected with the perfection of the cuisine. Little dinners, pretty and enjoyable, are, to my mind, the only rational way of entertaining. If people in ordinary circumstances are to make them a success, they must try no elaborate dishes, no long dinners which it is necessary to get some one in to cook, for this is always evident, and makes dinner-giving both a burden and an expense. If little dinners are to be successful, they must be free from all unnecessary labor and expenditures, otherwise they lapse into long dinners, too often stupid, with the hostess too wearied to be bright, after a day spent in a hot kitchen, helping her incompetent cook to struggle with unaccustomed, and hence, difficult dishes. As one course after another comes on, their success is her chief anxiety, rather than the entertainment of her guests. The dishes may be fewer at the home dinner. Let the guest who is invited to your home feel that you are not making an extra effort in his behalf, a knowledge which makes a guest feel most uncomfortable. On the contrary, let them feel that you are dispensing your every-day hospitality, and that they are heartily welcome.

An eminent authority on housekeeping says: "Let no one suppose that, because she lives in a small house and dines on homely fare, the general principles here laid down do not apply to her. Taste may be quite as well displayed in the arrangement of dishes on a pine table, as in grouping the silver and china of the rich. Skill in cooking is as readily shown in a baked potato or a johnny cake, as in a canvas-back duck. The charm will lie in nice attention to little things, not in a superabundance."

11

Much tact is necessary in choosing the guests for an informal dinner. It is so difficult to invite, or rather select those whom you know will harmonize. As the intercourse is free and social, only agreeable elements should be brought together.

A family dinner, even with a few friends, can be made quite attractive and satisfactory without much display or expense; consisting first, of good soups, then fish, garnished with suitable additions, followed by a roast; then vegetable, and some made dishes, a salad, crackers, cheese and olives; then dessert. This sensible meal, well cooked and neatly served, will please one, and is within the means of any housekeeper in ordinary circumstances.

Coffee and tea are served lastly, poured into tiny cups, and served clear, passed away on a tray to each guest, then sugar and cream passed, that each person may be allowed to season to suit himself.

Dinner given by those who love to entertain, should be made as elegant as possible, and complete in all its points. The first step is to study those simple customs whose observance makes them charming.

To make a dinner as good as possible does not imply a great outlay of money, but the observation of the most simple rules of table decoration which is one half of a Dinner.

HOW TO PLEASE HUSBANDS.

A good many husbands are utterly spoiled by mismanagement. Some women go about as if they were bladders and blow them up. Others keep them constantly in hot water. Others let them freeze by carelessness and indifference. Some keep them in a stew by irritating ways and words. Others roast them. Some keep them in a pickle all their lives. It can not be expected that any husband will be good and tender managed in that way, but they are really delicious when properly treated.

In selecting a husband you should not be guided by the silvery appearance, as in buying a mackerel, nor by the golden tint, as if you wanted a salmon. Be sure to select him yourself, as tastes differ.

Do not go to market for him as the best are always brought to your door. It is far better to have none unless you patiently learn to cook him.

A preserving kettle of finest porcelain is best, but an earthen pipkin will do, with care. See that the linen in which you wrap him is nicely washed and mended, with the required number of buttons and strings tightly sewed on.

Tie him in the kettle by a strong silk cord called Comfort, as the one called Duty is weak. Make a clear, steady fire of love, neatness and cheerfulness. Set him as near this as seems to agree with him.

Don't be anxious if he sputters and fizzes, for some do this till they are quite done. Add a little sugar known to confectioners as kisses, but no vinegar under any circumstances.

A little spice improves him, but must be used with judgement. Don't stick any sharp instrument into him to see if he is becoming tender. Stir gently, watching the while, lest he lie too close to the the kettle and so become useless. You can not fail to know when he is done.

If thus treated you'll find him relishing, agreeing nicely with you and children. He will keep as long as you want, unless you become careless and set him in a cold place.

THE FOLLOWING LIST OF NAMES REPRESENTS
CINCINNATI'S MOST PROMINENT AND
SUCCESSFUL CONCERNS

14

Inasmuch as this book, full of useful
information for the new housewife is
given to you gratis:—

We would appreciate your favoring
the advertisers herein who pay for
its maintainance.

THE F. C. H. MANNS CO.
PUBLISHERS

CINCINNATI, OHIO

General Index
Of
Recipes and Household Hints.

A

D

¶

J

K

L

M

ℜ

◍

ℙ

T

V

W

COMPRESSED YEAST BREAD.

To each part of luke-warm liquid, composed of equal portions of sweet milk and water, add a teaspoon of salt, and one-half ounce cake of compressed yeast dissolved in about three tablespoons of cold water, then stir in flour with a spoon until a dough is formed sufficiently stiff to turn from the mixing bowl in a mass. Put the dough on a moulding board and knead well, adding flour until it ceases to stick to the fingers or board, then put it in a well greased earthen bowl, brush the surface lightly with melted butter to keep it from crusting, cover with a bread cloth; set to rise and let stand for three hours at a temperature of 75 degrees, then form into loaves and put into greased pans; brush the top with melted butter or drippings; cover and again set to rise for an hour at the same temperature. When light enough to bake, it should be double the size in bulk it was when set to rise, and should be so aerated all through that when lifted in the pan the sense of weight will be scarcely perceptible.

BOSTON BROWN BREAD.

One pint Indian meal (yellow), half-pint rye meal, or Graham if you cannot get rye; one teaspoon salt, one full spoon soda, one cup New Orleans molasses. Add enough sour milk or buttermilk to make the mixture as thin as you would make griddle-cake batter. Steam three hours, then set it in the oven a little while to dry.

BROWN BREAD.

One pint sour milk, one teaspoonful soda, half pint molasses, two pints Graham flour; bake two hours in two buttered tin cans with buttered paper on top.

CANADA GINGER BREAD.

One cup butter, two cups sugar, one cup molasses, three eggs, one nutmeg, and one tablespoon ginger, one pound currants, one teacup milk, one tablespoon cinnamon, five cups flour, one teaspoon soda or two teaspoons baking powder.

25

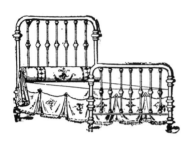

WHEN BUYING OUR MAKE

BRASS BEDS

FROM YOUR DEALER, WE FULLY GUARANTEE THEM

DON'T BE LED TO BUY ANY OTHER

WE ALSO

REPAIR AND RELACQUER BRASS BEDS

TRY OUR

PERFECTION SPRING

90 DAYS FREE TRIAL

NUNNER & ASHTON

FACTORY, 210 E. PEARL STREET

TELEPHONE M. 3496   CINCINNATI, O.

BOSTON BROWN BREAD.

One teacup of meal, two teacups of Graham flour, one cup of molasses, one cup of sweet milk, one teaspoon soda beaten in the molasses, one teaspoon salt. Mix ingredients well and place in tins with covers; put in roasting pan containing three pints of water and put in oven; let it remain two and one-half hours; remove the cans and covers and return to oven to dry about twenty minutes.

BROWN BREAD.

One cup New Orleans molasses, put one teaspoonful soda in the molasses after it has been warmed on the stove and dissolved, put in one cup sour milk or buttermilk, one cup corn meal, butter the size of an egg and one teaspoonful of salt; stir into this enough Graham flour to make stiff batter; beat light; put in greased pans; steam three hours. Bake in oven 20 minutes.

CORN BREAD.

One and one-half cups corn meal, half cup flour, butter size of an egg, two teaspoons of baking powder, one egg, one teaspoon salt, five tablespoons sugar, one pint of milk. Bake one-half hour.

OATMEAL BREAD.

One pint oatmeal scalded in one quart boiling water; when cool add one cupful of molasses with a very little soda, one-half yeast cake dissolved, teaspoonful of salt, two quarts flour; after it has risen the first time stir it a little with a knife, turn into the baking pans and let rise the second time. Do not knead it and bake in a moderate oven.

GINGER BREAD

Two eggs, one teacup New Orleans molasses' one teacup buttermilk, one-half teacup lard, one-half teacup brown sugar, two level teapoons soda, one tablespoon of ginger. Flour enough fcr thin batter.

SOFT GINGERBREAD.

One cup butter, one cup molasses, one cup sour milk, one cup sugar, two and one-half cups flour, four eggs, one teaspoon cinnamon, one teaspoon ginger, two teaspoons soda. Bake in a deep pan.

A Beautiful Piano Book

FRUIT CAKE.

Two pounds butter, two pounds sugar (granulated), two pounds eggs (weighed in shell), three pounds stoned raisins, three pounds currants, one pound citron and lemon peel together, one-half ounce spice; flavor with lemon, also five drops oil of almonds, two and a half pounds flour, one teaspoon baking powder. Bake four hours.

BUCKWHEAT CAKES.

One-half cake yeast, two cups buckwheat, little salt, three table-spoons maple syrup, enough water to make a thin batter. Do not stir any the next morning before baking.

SOFT GINGER CAKE.

One-half cup of sugar, one cup each of butter, molasses, and boiling water; two teaspoons of soda, one egg, spice or ginger to taste, three teacups of sifted flour. Pour the boiling water on the soda; mix thoroughly and bake in a moderate oven.

GINGER COOKIES.

Two cups molasses, one cup sugar, one cup sour milk, one cup shortening, one tablespoonful soda, one teaspoonful ginger, one tea-spoon cinnamon, one-half teaspoon salt ; flour enough to roll.

HICKORYNUT CAKE.

One-half cup butter, one and one-third cups sugar, one-half cup sweet milk, two and one-half cups flour, three eggs, one cup hick-orynut meats, two teaspoonsful baking powder. Season with lemon.

COOKIES.

One teacup of white sugar, one-half teacup of butter, one egg, and two tablespoons of sour milk. Dissolve soda in hot water, and add enough to the sour milk to make it foam. Grate in a little nut meg. Roll thin and before cutting out sprinkle over a little coarse sugar, pass the rolling pin over softly to prevent callering. Cut out and bake.

DELMONICO CAKE.

One cup butter, two cups sugar, three eggs, four cups of flour, one cup water, two teaspoons baking powder, one teaspoon vanilla. Bake in layers.

FILLING FOR SAME.

Three cups brown sugar, three-fourth cup cream or milk, butter size of walnut, one and one-half tablespoons flour, mixed thorougly in sugar, one and one-half teaspoons vanilla. Let boil until it begins to thicken or will hair when dripping from the spoon. Let cool before putting between layers. Be careful not to let it burn.

ANGEL CAKE.

The whites of nine eggs beaten to a stiff froth; add one-half teaspoonful cream of tartar to whites of eggs while beating them; add one and one-fourth cup of granulated sugar and one of flour. Sift sugar once, flour four times. Bake in ungreased pans 45 or 50 minutes.

GOLD CAKE.

A scant half cup butter, one cup sugar; cream together until light; add yolks, of eight eggs beaten light, one-half cup milk, one and one half cup flour, two teaspoonsful baking powder.   Bake 45 or 50 minutes.

GOLD CAKE

One cup sugar, three-fourth cup butter, one-half cup milk, one and one-half cups flour, yolks of eight eggs, two teaspoonsful baking powder. lemon flavor. Bake in same way as White Cake and ice with white icing; make from confectioner's sugar; flavor with lemon.

WHITE CAKE.

Whites of eight eggs, two cups sugar, one scant cup butter' one cup milk or water, three cups flour, two teaspoonsful Royal baking powder, vanilla flavor.   Cream the butter and sugar; then stir in all of the milk or water gradually; then the beaten whites; the flour with baking powder last.   Bake in oblong dripping pan.   Ice with Chocolate.

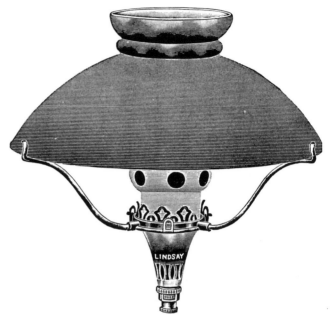
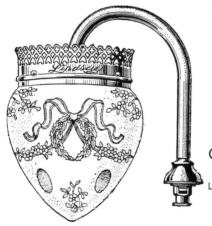

SNOW CAKE.

One and one-half cups sugar, two-thirds cup butter, cream together and flavor; one-half cup milk, one cup flour; mix well then add one-half cup milk and two of flour, two teaspoons baking powder, little salt, five stiff whites of eggs. Icing: one and one-half cups of sugar, one-half cup water, boil till it drops in threads from a spoon; stiff whites of two eggs, one-third teaspoon cream of tartar, vanilla to taste, beat till thick.

MARSHMALLOW CAKE.

Eighteen eggs (whites only), two and one-fourth cups of powdered sugar, one and one-half cups of flour, two teaspoons cream of tartar, one teaspoon vanilla or almond; sift sugar twice. Beat eggs very light, then cut sugar in with a broad bladed knife; sift flour four or five times after adding cream of tartar; cut it into sugar, beat, add vanilla. Bake in three layer in ungreased pans, with light brown paper in bottom of pan. Filling: boil two cups of sugar with one cup of water until it spins a thread; cut one-half pound of marshmallows fine, add just before taking off, let them melt, then pour this mixture slowly into the well beaten whites of two eggs, beat until cold, then put between layers. This filling can be used with the ordinary angle food by baking it in layers.

LADY CAKE

Two and one half scant cups flour, after sifting, mix well with one heaping teaspoonful baking powder, add one and one-half teacupfuls powdered sugar blended with one-half teacup of butter; beat whites of two eggs to froth; add gradually to the flour one-half teacup milk; follow with sugar and butter and next whites of eggs and one teaspoon of essence of almond, if desired.

CREAM CAKE.

One cup sugar, one cup flour, one teaspoonful baking powder (or one-half teaspoonful soda, with one teaspoonful cream tartar) flavor. Beat two eggs in a teacup, and fill same with sweet cream.

WILLIAM HENRY HARRISON.

Garfield Park Cincinnati, Ohio.

GINGER CAKE.

One cup molasses, one-half cup melted butter stirred in, one egg, one teaspoonful ginger, one and one-half cups of flour, one-half cup boiling water, one teaspoonfultof soda.

METROPOLITAN CAKE.

Two cups sugar, one of butter, one of milk, nearly four cups flour whites of eight eggs, three teaspoons baking powder flavor with lemon. Take alittle more than three-fifth of this mixture in three jelly pans ; add to the rmaining batter one tablespoon ground allspice, one and a half tablespoons cinnamon, teaspoon cloves, fourth pound each of sliced citron and chopped raisins ; bake in two jelly tins ; put together with frosting, alternating dark and light.

MINNEHAHA CAKE

One and a half cup of sugar, half cup of butter, stirred to a cream; whites of six eggs, or three whole eggs; two teaspoons baking powder stirred in two heaping cups sifted flour. For filling, take a tea cup sugar and a little water boiled together until it is brittle when dropped in cold water; remove from stove, stir quickly into the well beaten white of an egg ; add to this a cup of stoned raisins chopped fine, or a cup of chopped nuts, and place between layers and over top.

FROSTING WITH GELATINE.

Dissolve large pinch gelatine in six tablespoons boiling water; strain and thicken with sugar and flavor with lemon. This is enough for two cakes.

CHOCOLATE CAKE.

Yolks of eight eggs or four whole eggs, beat fifteen minutes; add cup of water, two of sugar, three of flour, two teaspoons baking powder, vanilla. If four eggs are used beat the whites separately and add just before putting in oven.

FILLING.

One cup of grated bitter chocolate, one cup of granulated sugar, tablespoon butter, cream to moisten.

MARBLE CAKE.
WHITE PART.

One cup white sugar, one-half cup of butter, one cup milk, whites of four eggs, one teaspoon lemon, two teaspoons baking powder, three cups flour.

DARK PART.

One cup sugar, one-half cup butter, one cup milk, yolks four eggs, three cups flour, one-half nutmeg, one-half teaspoon allspice, one-half teaspoon cinnamon, two teaspoon baking powder.

CINNAMON CAKE.

One pint of water, one cent yeast, one tablespoon sugar, one-half teaspoon salt, flour to make a batter. When it raises add one cup sugar, one-half cup milk, one tablespoon lard, two eggs; flour to make as thich as cake; drop dough in pans about one inch thick: when raised sift cinnamon and granulated sugar, and drop small lumps of butter over top. Cook in quick oven fifteen minutes.

FRUIT CAKES.

Two pounds currants, two pounds raisins, one pound citron, one pound dates, one pound flour, grate the inside of one five cent loaf of bread; one pound brown sugar, one pound soft shelled almonds, blanched; three-quarters pounds butter, ten eggs, two-thirds cup black coffee, two nutmegs, one teaspoon cinnamon, one teaspoon allspice, one teaspoon cloves. Bake three and a half hours, steady heat.

STRAW BERRY SHORT CAKE.

One quart flour, three tablespoons of butter, one large cup of sour cream, one egg, one large tablespoon of sugar, one teaspoon soda dissovled in warm water and a little salt. Rub the shortning into the the salted flour; add the egg and soda to the milk, then put all together, handling slightly. Roll lightly and quickly into two crusts one-half inch thick; lay one on the other and bake; while warm separate them and lay upon the lower crust a thick coating of fruit, sprinkling with powdered sugar, and lay on the upper crust. Serve with sweetened milk or cream.

DELICATE CAKE.

Two even cups of sugar, one-half cup of butter. beatən to a cɪeam three-fourths of a cup of milk, two even cups of flour, (sift thrice), one teaspoon cream tartar, one-half teaspoon soda, whites of six eggs, beaetn very light· Stir in soda last.

SUNSHINE CAKE.

Add the yolks of two or more eggs to the mixture for Angel Food just before sifting in the flour.

ANGEL CAKE.

One cup of white of eggs, one heaping cup of winter wheat flour, one and one-half cups of fine granulated sugar, one level teaspoon of cream of tartar, one teaspoonful of almond extract. (Eggs vary so much in sixe it is better to take a certain measure of the white.) Put the measured whites in an earthen bowl ; break lightly with an egg whip, sift in the cream of tartar and beat until the egg will cling to the bowl and not slip out when turned upside down ; then beat the sugar into the egg, sifting it gradually, adding the flavor, and lastly, sift in the flour, stirring only enough to combine it with the sugar and egg. Put the mixture in an ungreased pan, the bottom of which has been covered with white paper, place carefully in an oven of moderate temperature and cover with a baking sheet or tin so as to protect the top of cake, but not exclude the air. Remove the cover in half an hour when the cake should be perfectly risen; bake half an hour longer; when taken from the oven turn pan bottom upwards, and if it has no center tube, rest it upon cups until the cake is perfectly cold, then remove by slipping a thin knife between the cake and sides of the pan. Success depends largely upon having the oven the proper temperature; if too warm, the cake will be tough.

WHITE CAKE.

Whites of eleven eggs, two cups sugar, one cup butter, one-half cup milk, three cups flour three teaspoonsful baking powder, one teaspoonful vanilla.

HONORABLE WILLIAM HOWARD TAFT.
PRESIDENT OF THE UNITED STATES
A Cincinnati Product.

PEACH SHORTCAKE.

Take one quart nice peaches, cut and sugar to taste. Set aside for cake. One heaping half pint flour sifted twice, a saltspoon of salt, one teaspoon baking powder, piece of butter size of a walnut. Mix quickly and lightly with enough milk to make a dough like bread. Use a fork for mixing; put in a greased pan, smooth over with fork; bake in a quick oven 15 minutes; take out, split, and spread peaches between; cover all with a tin pan, return to oven for 10 minutes before serving.

POOR MAN'S FRUIT CAKE.

One and one-half cups brown sugar, two cups flour, one cup butter, one cup chopped raisins, three eggs, three tablespoons sour milk, one-half teaspoon soda, one-half cup blackberry jam. Mix eggs, butter and sugar together first, then flour and milk and fruit; then add one-half teaspoon cloves, cinnamon, and one-half of a nutmeg.

BLACKBERRY CAKE.

One cup brown sugar, three-fourths cup butter, three eggs, three tablespoons sour cream, one and one-half cups blackberry jam, three cups flour, one teaspoon soda, one-half nutmeg, tablespoon cinnamon. Bake in layers, and put icing between layers.

ALMOND CREAM CAKE.

Two cups powdered sugar, full half cup butter, three-quarter cup sweet milk, two and a half cups sifted flour, two teaspoonsful baking powder, pinch of salt, whites of six eggs, teaspoon of vanilla. Beat butter and sugar until very light; add milk slowly, then flour into which the baking powder has been stirred; last, add whites of eggs, with pinch of salt, beaten stiff, and vanilla. Bake in two thick layers.

FOR CREAM.

Take one-half pint sweet cream, whipped stiff; one-half pound almonds, blanched and chopped fine; teaspoon vanilla, and sugar to taste. Stir all together and put between layers, after they have first been coated with boiled icing.

41

CUSTARD CAKE.

Three eggs, one cup sugar, one and one-half cups flour, two teaspoons baking powder, a little salt, bake in two round tins; when cold split open and fill with custard.

CUSTARD.

Put one pint sweet milk in a double boiler; when hot stir in one cup sugar, one-half cup corn starch, two eggs, all creamed together.

CARAMEL ICING.

Two cups light brown sugar, one-half cup milk; one-half cup butter; boil together until you can form in balls when put in cold water; then add two tablespoonsful of chocolate. Take from fire and beat until thick enough to spread on cake.

COOKIES.

One cup sugar, one cup butter, one-third cup of milk, two eggs, two teaspoonsful of baking powder, nutmeg.

MARBLE CAKE.
LIGHT PART.

One and one-half cups granulated sugar, one-half cup butter, whites four eggs, one-half cup sour milk, one-quarter teaspoonful soda, two cups sifted flour.

DARK PART.

One cup sugar, one-half cup molasses, one-half cup butter, one-half cup sour milk, yolks four eggs, one-quarter teaspoonful soda, two cups sifted flour, one tablespoon cinnamon; one-half grated nutmeg.

DELMONICO CAKE.

One and one-half cups sugar, one cup butter, one cup sweet milk, three cups flour, one heaping tablespoonful baking powder, the whites of six eggs beaten to a stiff froth; flavor to taste and bake in layers.

CARAMEL FILLING.

Four cups New Orleans brown sugar, two cups cream, two tablespoonsful of butter; boil together until thick, and stir until cold; flavor with vanilla and spread on cake layers.

ICE CREAM CAKE.

Three eggs beaten separately (use whites), one-half cup butter, one cup powdered sugar, one and one-half cup flour, one teaspoon baking powder, one teaspoon vanilla. Bake in layers.

FILLING.

Beat the yolks of the three eggs and one cup of powdered sugar for twenty minutes; add one teaspoon vanilla.

JAM CAKE.

Two cups of sugar, one-half cup of butter, four eggs, (add whites well beaten last of all); four cups of flour, one cup blackberry jam or jelly, in half cup of sour milk; one teaspoon of cinnamon, one teaspoon ground cloves, one teaspoon of nutmeg. Bake in layers; put icing on each layer and sprinkle nuts between. (Any kind of jam or jelly will answer).

ICE CREAM CAKE.

Make good sponge cake, bake half an inch thick in jelly pans, and let them get perfectly cold; take a pint of thickest sweet cream, beat until it looks like ice cream, make very sweet, and flavor with vanilla; blanch and chop one pound almonds, stir into cream, and put very thick between each layer.

SPONGE CAKE.

Twelve eggs, beaten separate, leaving out three yolks; two even tin cups of sugar, two heaping tin cups of flour, one-half cup of cold water, juice and rind of one lemon.

WHITE CAKE.

Whites of eleven eggs, two cups sugar, one cup butter, one-half cup milk, three cups flour, three teaspoons baking powder, one teaspoonful vanilla.

SNOW-DRIFT CAKE.

One cup butter, two cups sugar, one cup milk, whites of six eggs, four cups flour, two teaspoonsful baking powder. Flavor with lemon.

46

CREAM CAKE.

Three eggs, three-quarters cup of sugar, one cup of flour, one and one-half teaspoons baking powder.

CREAM F R LAYER.

One tablespoonful of butter, one pint of milk, one-half cup of sugar, one egg, one tablespoonful corn starch; also a little salt, flavor with vanilla, and cook until thick, stiring constantly; spread on cake layers while hot.

FRUIT CAKE.

One and one-half pounds of raisins, one and one-half pounds of currants, one-quarter pound citron, one teaspoonful of cloves, one of cinnamon, and one of allspice, one cupful of dark molasses, one-half pound of butter, one orange and the rind grated; one-half cup of sour milk, with one-half teaspoonful of soda. Brown two cups of flour in the oven. One cup of white flour mixed with the fruit; three eggs and one cup of granulated sugar. Stir the butter and sugar together, add the eggs, molasses and the rest of the recipe. Bake in a large pan three hours in a slow oven.

SNOW CAKE.

One-half cup butter, one cup pulverized sugar, one and one-half cups of flour, one-half cup sweet milk, whites of four eggs, one teaspoonful baking powder.

BLACKBERRY JAM CAKE.

One and one-half cups blackberry jam, six tablespoons sour milk, three cups flour, two teaspoons soda, two grated nutmegs, two teaspoons allspice and cinnamon, one cup butter, two cups sugar, six eggs. Bake in four layers.

WHITE LAYER CAKE
WITH SOUR ICING.

Two cups granulated sugar, not quite full; whites of seven eggs, one even cup of butter, one cup of milk, two heaping teaspoons baking powder, three and one-half cups of flour (after having sifted), one teaspoon vanilla, add whites of eggs last.

CITY HALL OF CINCINNATI, OHIO.

DEDICATED 1891

MAYONAISE DRESSING.

Three-fourth cup of vinegar, one tablespoon of butter; boil this and set aside. Then add two teaspoons prepared mustard, one-fourth spoon pepper, one-half spoon celery and mustard seed (whole). Beat yolks of two eggs, one tablespoon sugar, one of sweet cream together, then mix with vinegar and butter and boil three minutes.

MAYONAISE DRESSING.

One tablespoon of Coleman's mustard, three yolks of eggs, one saltspoon of salt, dash of cayenne pepper, juice of one lemon, three-fourths pint of olive oil, teaspoon tarragon vinegar; beat yolks and add mustard, stir in oil gradually, then salt and pepper; when about one-half oil is in put in vinegar; lastly, juice of lemon. Make one and one-half hour before using, and place on ice to get firm.

MAYONAISE.

Yolks of three eggs beaten, one teaspoon mustard, two teaspoons salt, one-fourth saltspoon cayenne pepper, two tablespoons sugar, two tablespoons melted butter or oil, one cup cream or milk, one-half cup *hot* vinegar, whites of three eggs beaten stiff. Cook in double broiler until it thickens like soft custard. Stir well.

MAYONAISE DRESSING.

One cup vinegar, let boil and then add beaten yolk of three eggs, one teaspoon salt, one teaspoon ground mustard, one teaspoon sugar, one teaspoon cornstarch which has been dissolved in a little milk, one cup of milk (mixed with all the above ingredients but the vinegar), then add to the hot vinegar and let the whole come to a boil. When taken off add a teaspoon of butter.

MUSTARD.

One-half cup cugar, one egg, one tablespoon mustard. Beat together, then add one-half cup vinegar. Boil until it thickens.

POTTER'S
18-20-22-24 W. FIFTH ST.,
CINCINNATI, OHIO

THE GREAT HOME SHOE STORE OF THE QUEEN CITY, WE BEGAN FITTING CINCINNATI PEOPLE IN SHOES IN 1866 AND SLOWLY, BUT SURELY, OUR BUSINESS HAS GROWN TO BE THE

LARGEST IN THE MIDDLE WEST.

ISN'T THIS THE BEST EVIDENCE THAT OUR CUSTOMERS HAVE BEEN WELL TREATED?

MAYONAISE DRESSING.

Boil together three-fourth pint vinegar, one-half cup sugar, one-half cup butter, yolk of four eggs, mixed with four tablespoons of milk, one-half teaspoon of salt, pepper and ground mustard. Stir all together and pour on boiling vinegar and butter. Boil for three minutes and put in self-sealing jar.

WALDORF SALAD.

Pare, core and cut into dice four large tart apples ; add to them a quart of celery cut into half inch pieces. Dust over a teaspoon salt, a teaspoon paprika and two tablespoons tarragon vinegar. Mix all together and stir in a cup and one-half stiff mayonaise.

SALAD CREAM.

1. One medium sized boiled potato rubbed very smooth; beat in yolks of two raw eggs, add desert spoon each of salt and fine sugar, and add cayenne pepper to taste.

2. Yolks of two hard boiled eggs, rubbed very smooth ; add desert spoonful of nice mustard, and rub the egg and mustard well together.

3. Mix 1 and 2 thoroughly together and then add olive oil in small quantities, and stir it in thoroughly as long as the mixture continues to thicken ; then add vinegar till it is as thin as desired. Be sure to heat the oil in thoroughly, a little at a time, or it will not mix well. This is excellent for chicken or lobster salad.

SALAD DRESSING.

One cup butter, one-half cup sugar ; cream together, and then add one tablespoon salt, one tablespoon ground dry mustard, pinch cayenne pepper, yolks of six eggs, one cup cream, either sweet or sour ; put this when mixed into one pint boiling vinegar and cook till thick. Add extract celery or celery salt for potato salad. This dressing makes one quart and may be kept a long time if put in mason jar and kept cool. For Lettuce, Cabbage or Potato Salad.

JVenture to say that if you follow this advice for a few years, you will send me a letter of thanks for putting it in this book.

Commence your house-keeping by being economical. The watching of the household expenses is a very important item in most peoples lives. There is no way in which you can save as much as by buying your groceries and meats at one of the

KROGER GROCERY & BAKING CO'S. STORES,

where you have to pay cash. This takes away the temptation of buying more things than you can afford. In running a book, you will frequently buy some little extravagant things because you buy on credit, and you also buy them at a higher price.

If you will save something every week, and put it in a savings bank and allow it to accumulate with interest, you will be be able to buy your own home, but don't buy it until you have enough money to pay for it. Then you have again the advantage of being able to buy for cash, and buy any snap trade that is offered.

If you have your home paid for, or if you don't want to buy a home you may have enough to start in business, and after this is accomplished, your surplus earnings can be put into city bonds, which are the safest form of investment, and the re-investment of the interest every year will in time accumulate for you a competency that will keep you comfortable in your old age.

B. H. KROGER, President

The Kroger Grocery & Baking Co.

BROILED OYSTERS.

Take the number of oysters desired and drain off the liquor; dip them each one separately in cracker dust to which has been added some salt. Put them on a broiler that has been greased and broil two minutes on each side. Serve on hot toast with any sauce desired, or slices of lemon on which has been sprinkled dried parsley finely broken up.

CORN OYSTERS.

One dozen ears of corn, three eggs, three or four large crackers rolled very fine, one tablespoon sugar, one-half teaspoon of salt, one dash of pepper. Score the corn and press out the pulp with the back of a knife. Beat the eggs separately and add the whites just as you are ready to fry the oysters.

FRIED SOFT SHELL CRABS.

Take as many soft shell crabs as needed and wash thoroughly. Dip each one in flour and then in egg (the whites and yolks beaten together with a teaspoon of water), and then in cracker crumbs. Have your lard very hot and drop in the crabs. Let them fry for five minutes. Drain off all fat and sprinkle a little salt over each one. Serve on hot toast. Garnish with lemon and parsley, and on the side a teaspoon of tartar sauce.

BROILED SARDINES ON TOAST.

Take ten good sized sardines which are whole. Place them on a toaster or double broiler and let toast two minutes on each side; have the fire brisk. Serve on hot toast with lemon cut in quarters, and sprigs of parsley laid around each piece of toast.

VEAL LOAF.

Two pounds veal, one-half pound pickle pork, one teaspoon pepper, two teaspoons salt, sage to taste. Beat one egg in cup, fill cup with milk, leaving in egg; add six tablespoons rolled crackers, then make in loaf and roll in crackers. Bake one hour.

SPANISH CREAM.

Dissolve one-half box gelatine in pint of milk; boil and add the yolks of two eggs, beaten with one-half teacup of sugar. When it comes to a boil, remove from fire and add the whites of eggs beaten to a froth. Flavor to taste.

CREAM SALMON.

One can salmon minced fine. drain off liquor, throw away. For the dressing boil one pint milk, two tablespoons butter; salt and pepper to taste. Have ready one pint fine bread crumbs, place in a layer in the bottom of dish, then a layer of fish, then dressing and so on, having crumbs for the last layer. Bake until brown.

CREAM PUFFS.

Half cup butter melted in one cup hot water ; put on to boil; while boiling, stir in one cup of flour; when cold add three eggs and stir until smooth. Drop into muffin pans and bake 30 or 40 minutes. Filling : two cups milk, two eggs, one cup sugar, little corn starch, vanilla to taste. This makes 12,

POTATO PUFFS.

One cup mashed potatoes, one teaspoon of butter, one egg, one-half cup of cream. Salt and pepper to taste. Beat the egg light, white and yolk separately, then melt butter; add to potato with the cream. Season and beat until light. Fill greased pop-over pans and bake in a quick oven. Serve at once on a heated dish.

APPLE FRITTERS.

First core and then pare three or four apples, but do not break them; cut them into slices one-third of an inch thick, leaving the opening in the centre; dip each slice in fritter batter, fry in hot fat, same as doughnuts; bananas can be used. Fritter batter: yolks of two eggs beaten well, add half cup of milk and one tablespoonful of olive oil, a little salt and one cup of flour; when ready to use add the whites of the eggs, beaten very stiff; also add one teaspoonful of sugar.

RUBEN R. SPRINGER.

One Of Cincinnati's Benefactors.

CELERY SOUP.

One cup celery, two onions, one pint water, big lump butter, salt, and pepper; boil till nearly dry and very tender; add one pint milk and a little flour to thicken, and strain.

POTATO SOUP.

Three medium sized potatoes, one and one-half tea cups of water, three cups of milk, one and one-half teaspoons of flour, two thin slices of onion. Cook potatoes soft, drain and mash fine; scald the onion in the milk, then add the mashed potatoes. Melt the butter in a sauce pan, stir in the flour and add to the soup; add the one and one-half cups of hot water; stir well, until flour is cooked thoroughly; then strain through a colandar.

TOMATO SOUP.

One cooking spoon of sugar, one can, or one dozen large tomatoes cut fine, one quart of warm water. Cook rather slowly until the tomatoes are soft enough to mash fine, put through fine sieve all that can be strained through, mix two cooking spoons of flour with one of butter (melted); add pint of milk—cream is better; heat, then add tomatoes, boil three or four minutes, serve. If milk is not liked, leave it out, adding water instead. If onions are liked, cut one medium sized one into the tomotoes when first cooked and before straining. Celery can be used either in place of, or with the onions, or cut fine and added with the milk.

BISQUE OF TOMATO SOUP.

Take one can of tomatoes and cook until thick. Put through a strainer. Put one quart of milk into a double boiler and let boil. While the milk is boiling stir in the tomatoes; quickly add your seaoning (salt, pepper and butter), and then add a pinch of soda; this will cause the soup to foam, but it will soon settle down. Do not put the tomatoes in the milk until you are ready to serve the soup, as it is not good if left standing. If fresh tomatoes are used, have enough to make two scant cups after cooking and straining. The tomatoes must always be cooked before making this soup.

FIRST OF ALL

LET US CONGRATULATE YOU MOST HEARTILY!
THEN INTRODUCE OURSELVES, WE ARE

THE ❧ ❧ BODEN ART EMPORIUM

1152 MAIN STREET   CINCINNATI, O.

DEALERS
IN
PICTURES
AND
ART
N
O
V
E
L
T
I
E
S

FINE
FRAMING
AND
REGILD-
ING

OUR
S
P
E
C
I
A
L
T
Y

THEN WE WANT TO GIVE YOU A WEDDING PRESENT.
BRING IN YOUR MARRIAGE CERTIFICATE AND WE WILL
FRAME IT NICELY,

ABSOLUTELY FREE

OF CHARGE.   DO NOT HESITATE WE WANT TO GET
ACQUAINTED.

MIXED PICKLES.

One quart small cucumbers, one quart large cucumbers cut fine, one quart small onions, one quart string beans, one quart small green tomatoes, three green peppers, one large cauliflower. Put all in salt water twenty-four hours; place in porcelain kettle and bring to a boil in clear water. Paste: Two-thirds cup of flour, six tablespoons ground mustard, six tablespoons sugar, one tablespoon tumeric, one quart vinegar. Place on a slow fire until thick, then pour over pickles while hot.

MIXED PICKLES.

One quart small cucumbers, one quart onions, one quart string beans, one large cauliflower, three green peppers with seed sout. Soak all in salt water twenty-four hours, then scald in same water till tender. Six tablespoons of flour, one tablespoon of tumeric, six tablespoons ground mustard, ten tablespoons sugar, one quart vinegar. Mix mustard, flour, sugar and tumeric with some of cold vinegar. Boil all together and pour over pickles.

MUSTARD PICKLES.

One quart small whole cucumbers, one quart large sliced cucumbers, one quart green tomatoes sliced, one quart small button onions, one large cauliflower divided into flowerets, and four green peppers cut fine. Make a brine of four quarts of water and one pint of salt, pour it over the mixture of vegetables and let it soak twenty-four hours. Heat just enough to scald it, and turn into a colander to drain. Mix one cup flour, six tablespoons of ground mustard, and one tablespoon of tumeric with enough cold vinegar to make a smooth paste; then add one and one-half cups of sugar, one-half cup of celery seeds, two tablespoons white mustard seed, and enough vinegar to make two quarts in all. Boil this mixture until it thickens and is smooth, stirring all the time, then add the vegetables and cook until well heated through. Put in Mason jars.

MAYONAISE DRESSING.

Two tablespoons of sugar, one tablespoon of flour, one cup of vinegar, one egg, salt and pepper, a little mustard and a tablespoon of butter. Mix the flour and mustard with a little water. Cook until thick.

MAYONAISE DRESSING.

The yolks of two eggs, a pinch of salt, one of mustard, cayenne pepper and sugar; beat this well. Now commence adding the oil, a very little at a time, beating in one direction all the time until the dressing is quite thick. Now add the vinegar a little at a time until you use about one tablespoonful, next add the juice of one-half a lemon. This is a very good dressing over lettuce. For chicken salad chop up about equal parts of chicken and celery, adding the dressing just before serving.

DRESSING. (BOIL.)

Four eggs, one and one-half tablespoons sugar, one-half pint vinegar; butter, size of an egg; salt to taste, pinch of pepper.

POTATO SALAD.

One pint sour cream, six hard boiled eggs, one and one-half teaspoons mustard, one teaspoon each of salt and pepper, two tablespoons sugar, one teaspoon cornstarch, one pt. vinegar, two eggs, three pints of cold boiled potatoes cut in small squares; take yolks of six boiled eggs, powder fine and make a paste with the two eggs; mix sugar, cornstarch, mustard, salt and peppeer dry, add enough cream to make a thin paste, then add the eggs, mix well, then add cream, then vinegar, mix well and boil; when done, chop whites of eggs, stir in. When cold pour over potatoes. More than one pint of cream can be used if liked, and more sugar. The potatoes ought to be boiled with jackets on, and the water in which they are boiled, salted.

CHICKEN SALAD.

One chicken; equal quantities chicken and celery; five hard boiled eggs.

PREPERATION FOR CLEANING CARPETS.

One cake of Ivory soap boiled in three gallons of water , four ounces soap tree bark boiled twenty minutes in a little water. Then add the strained bark juice and four ounces lump ammonia to the water and soap — splendid.

TO CLEAN KID GLOVES.

Cover with gasoline and let them stand two or three hours ; wash out and rinse in clean gasoline and rub with soft cloth until dry.

Sweet spirits of nitre and chloroform are both excellent for cleaning silk or wool goods.

LAKE WATER

Dont wash your face in ordinary lakewater. Put an ounce of powdered borax in a bottle and add a quart of water and the juice of two lemons. Whenever you wash your face put tablespoon of this lotion in the water.

HOUSEHOLD HINTS.

After wiping up the floor, while damp, sprinkle with common salt to keep away moths.

Open canned fruit an hour before bringing to tne table. It is far richer when the oxygen is thus restored to it.

All traces of mud can be removed from black clothes by rubbing the spots with raw potatoe.

Wash your knife in cold water after cutting onions to quickly remove the odor. Hot water causes it to linger about the knife.

AN OLD FASHIONED RECEIPT
FOR HOME COMFORT

Take of thought for self one part, two parts of thought for family equal parts of common sense and broad intelligence; a large modicum of the sense of the fitness of things, a heaping measure of living above what your neighbors think of you, twice the quantity of keeping within your income, sprinkling of what tends to refinement and asthetic beauty: stirring thick with Christian principle of the true brand and set to rise.

CINCINNATI'S ZOO—CLUB HOUSE AND BAND STAND.

ORANGE SAUCE.

One-half cup sugar, two cups of cream, juice of two oranges. Good for any pudding requiring cold sauce.

CHILI SAUCE.

Twenty-four large tomatoes, eight large onions, thirteen green sweet peppers, four cups vinegar, eight tablespoons sugar, four tablespoons salt, one teaspoon ginger, one teaspoon cloves, one teaspoon cinnamon, one red pepper. Cook three hours. Makes one gallon.

TOMATO SAUCE.

One quart can tomatoes, two tablespoons butter, two tablespoons flour, two cloves and a small slice of onion. Cook tomatoes, onions and cloves ten minutes. Heat the butter in a small frying pan and add the flour. When smooth and brown stir into the tomatoes and cook ten minutes. Season to taste with salt and pepper and rub through a strainer.

BORDEAUX SAUCE.

Two gallons of cabbage chopped fine, one gallon green tomatoes, one dozen onions chopped fine, one-half pound mustard seed, one ounce celery seed, one ounce black pepper, unground; one ounce cloves, one ounce allspices, one ounce tumeric, one gill salt, two pounds of brown sugar, one gallon cider vinegar. Boil *all* together twenty minutes. Keep from air.

TOMATO SAUCE.

One peck of tomatoes, nine large onions, two small peppers, one-cup half salt, eight cups vinegar, one cup sugar, nine teaspoons allspice, one and one-half teaspoons ginger, one and one-half teaspoons cloves, five teaspoons cinnamon. Boil two hours and bottle.

SAUCE.

Yolks of three eggs, three tablespoons of sugar, one pint of milk and cook to custard thickness.

CHICKEN SALAD.

Two chickens, three bunches celery (or cabbage). Dressing for same: Yolks of four eggs beaten well, twelve tablespoons vinegar, six tablespoons water, melted butter the size of a goose egg, one-half teaspoon mustard, one teaspoon sugar, salt and pepper. Stir mixture well and let boil until thickness of cream, then let cool before putting on chicken.

SALMON SALAD.

One can salmon, nine eggs boiled hard, one cup vinegar, one teaspoon salt, one teaspoon pepper, one teaspoon mustard. Pour the oil from the salmon, rub the yolks of eggs with the oil. Chop the fish fine and mix with the whites of eggs after they are chopped.

SALMON SALAD.

One can salmon; one-half dozen pickles chopped very fine, two bunches celery chopped fine, five hard boiled eggs chopped fine. Mustard, butter, pepper, salt and lemon juice to taste.

BEAT AND CABBAGE SALAD.

One quart sugar beats cooked and chopped fine, one quart raw cabbage, one cup sugar, one cup horse radish, grated; one tablespoon salt, one teaspoon pepper, one-half teaspoon red pepper. Cover with cold vinegar.

DRESSING.

One half cup milk, butter size of an egg, two-thirds cup vinegar, one tablespoon flour, three eggs, one tablespoon pepper, one teaspoon salt, one teaspoon mustard, two tablespoons sugar. Boil till consistency of cream.

POTATO SALAD.

Two eggs; beat the yolks then add one-half teaspoon mustard mixed with vinegar, one-half teaspoon pepper, one-half teaspoon salt, one teaspoon sugar, one-half cup vinegar, three tablespoons butter and a little cayenne pepper. Add the beaten whites, cook in a pan of water; when thick cool and add one-half cup sweet cream, one tablespoon chopped onion, one tablespoon celery. Slice potatoes and three hard boiled eggs, put alternate layers of potatoes and eggs.

ICING.

Two cups sugar, one cup cold water, one teaspoon vanilla. Boil the same as for boiled icing, and beat until cold.

BOILED ICING.

Two cups granulated sugar, one-quarter cup water; boil until this candies; then pour over whites of two well beaten eggs until it becomes stiff. Add juice of one lemon.

ICING.

Two teacups white sugar boiled until it threads, and whipped with the beaten whites of two eggs until it thickens. Spread between the layers and on top.

RASPBERRY ICE.

One quart of red raspberries, one pint of sugar, juice of two lemons, one quart of water, the whites of three eggs. Boil the sugar and water for five minutes. When cold add the raspberries and lemon juice, mashed. Strain through a cloth, pressing hard to extract the juice. Freeze.

LEMON ICE.

To the juice of three lemons add one pint of sugar. Let it dissolve well, then add slowly one quart of sweet milk, and then the whites of three eggs beaten stiff. Freeze.

LEMON FOAM.

Two cups of hot water, one cup of sugar, white; two large tablespoons of corn starch stirred into hot water and sugar. When slightly cool add juice of four lemons; beat all into whites of three eggs.

LEMON ICE.

One quart of milk, four lemons, two cups of sugar. Freeze milk a little, then put in the lemons and sugar. You will find this to be very good.

STRAWBERRY ICE.

One quart strawberry juice or crushed berries, one pint water, juice of two lemons. one pound granulated sugar, Freeze.

70

CREAM TAFFY.

Three cups granulated sugar, one-half cup vinegar, one-half cup water, butter size of walnut. Boil without stirring until it will candy when dropped in water. Flavor and pour on buttered tins. When cool pull until white, then cut into sticks with sharp shears.

COCOANUT CARAMELS.

One teacup of milk, butter size of an egg, one pint of grated cocoanut (dessicated may be used), four teacups light brown sugar, two teaspoons lemon. Boil slowly until stiff ; beat to a cream, pour into shallow pans. When partly cold cut in squares.

BUTTER SCOTCH.

One cup sugar, one cup molasses, one-half cup butter, one table-spoon vinegar, pinch of soda. Boil all together until done. Pour in buttered pans, cut in squares when cold and wrap in paraffine paper.

CARAMELS.

One-half cup chocolate, one-half cup milk, one cup molasses, two cups sugar, one-half cup butter, one teaspoon vanilla. Boil until it will harden in water : pour on platters and when nearly cold cut in squares.

CHOCOLATE CREAMS.

Three cups of sugar, two-thirds cup of water, one tablespoon vinegar. Boil until it hairs ; cool in a basin of water, stirring briskly. When cool, shape and roll in melted Baker's chocolate.

MINUET KISSES.

Buy the minuet crackers, they are thin and a little larger than a silver quarter, thus dainty. First, place a pan of these in a warming oven till crisp. Into a bowl break the white of an egg; be careful not to allow any of the yolk to get in; add one cupful of confection sugar, more if it does not form a soft paste. Spread each minuet with this, piling high in the center. Then press lightly the meat of an English walnut. Fill the pan and place in hot oven, watching constantly that they only come to a delicious brown.

J. G. SCHMIDLAPP

One Of Cincinnati's Benefactors.

SNOW PUDDING.

One-half box of Cox's gelatine, one and one-half pints of hot water (in summer one pint), one cup of sugar, one lemon, teaspoon vanilla, pinch of salt, stiff whites of three eggs. Serve with a custard, make with three yolks, cup sugar, pint milk, little vanilla.

GUESS PUDDING.

Boil one pound prunes till mushy, remove stones and strain, add one teaspoon of vanilla, pinch of salt, stiff whites of three eggs. Mix well and bake in a moderate oven till a light brown; serve with whipped cream.

PINE APPLE PUDDING.

Boil together two cups water, one cup sugar; dissolve three teaspoons corn starch, stir into the sugar and water. Beat the whites of three eggs until light, beat all together until cool; then stir in one box grated pine apple; eat with whipped cream or rich boiled custard.

GELATINE JELLY.

To one-half box gelatine add one-half pint cold water, let it stand two hours, when dissolved add the juice of two lemons, two oranges, and the grated rind of half a lemon, let it stand half an hour, then add one and a half pints of boiling water, one pound white sugar, one-half tumbler wine, and set it away to cool.

LEMON MERINGUE PUDDING.

One quart milk, two cups bread crumbs, four eggs, one-half cup of butter, one cup white sugar, one large lemon, use juice and half the rind grated. Soak the bread in the milk; add the beaten yolks of eggs with the butter and sugar rubbed to a cream; then add the lemon. Bake in buttered dish till slightly brown. Cover with a meringue of the whites whipped to a froth, with three teaspoons of powdered sugar and a little lemon juice. Brown very little, sift powdered sugar over it and serve hot.

LEMON PIE.

Make rich paste and bake shell first.

FILLING.

Grated rind and juice of one lemon, one cup sugar, one tablespoon flour mixed in sugar, one egg and yolk of two, one cup boiling water. Let boil until it thickens ; while still hot fill shell. Beat whites of two eggs to stiff froth ; add one tablespoonful sugar, spread over top of pie and place in oven until brown.

LEMON CREAM PIE.

One teacup sugar, one tablespoon butter, three eggs, save out whites of two ; juice of two and rind of one lemon, one cup of boiling water, one tablespoon of flour wet with cold water. Mix well and bake soft. Beat the whites with a little sugar, put on pie when nearly cold and brown lightly.

LEMON PIE.

For one pie take the juice and rind of one lemon, one cup of sugar, one tablespoon butter, one tablespoon corn starch, one cup hot water. Put on and let come to a boil ; when partly cold stir in the yolks of two eggs. Bake crusts separate, put in the mixture and make a meringue of the whites, and brown.

TWO LEMON PIES.

One cup sugar, one lemon, yolks of four eggs, one cup boiling water, one tablespoon flour. Bake crust first ; have whites of eggs for icing.

CREAM PIE.

Take one pint of milk and let in simmer on the stove with one teaspoon of butter in it, then mix the yolks of three eggs with one-half cup of sugar and one large spoon of corn starch softened in a little milk, and a pinch of salt. When the milk is hot add this, stirring constantly until smooth and thick. Flavor with lemon or vanilla. Bake your two under crusts and pinch the edges well ; when baked add the custard, then beat the whites of the three eggs well and add one-half cup of powdered sugar, spread on the custard and brown.

LEMON PIE.

Three lemons, rind and juice ; one and one-half cups sugar, two tablespoons flour, two cups of milk and the yolks of six eggs. After the pies are baked beat the six whites well and add one cup of powdered sugar ; spread on the top and brown. First mix the sugar, rinds and juice together, then add the yolks and flour, and last the milk. This will make two pies. Only grate the yellow of the lemons and remove seeds.

LEMON PIE.

Three eggs, one lemon, juice and rind ; one cup sugar, three tablespoons flour, one cup hot water. Take the white of one egg for frosting.

MINCE PIE.

Two pounds beef, two pounds currants, two pounds raisins, two pounds beef suet, one pound citron, one and one-half pounds candied lemon peel, four pounds apples, two pounds sugar, two grated nutmegs, one-fourth ounce cloves, one-fourth ounce mace, one-half ounce cinnamon, one teaspoon salt, two lemons, juice and rind ;two oranges, juice and rind. Simmer the meat gently till tender, and when cold chop fine. Stone raisins, shred citron, pare, core and chop apples and suet. Mix the dry ingredients, then add juice and rinds of oranges and lemons. Pack in a stone jar, cover close and keep cool. This meat will keep all winter. Cider can be added if so desired.

ELDERBERRY PIE.

One-half pint elderberries, one-half teacup sour cream, four tablespoons sugar, two tablespoons of flour; use two crusts.

VINEGAR PIE.

Yolks of three eggs, two tablespoons flour or cornstarch, (mix yolks and flour to paste) one cup sugar and one cup vinegar. Boil, stir in yolk mixture, then bake in one crust. Make frosting with the white of eggs and add to it a little lemon extract. Put on pie, then brown in oven. This will make two pies. If vinegar is too sour, add a little water. This is as nice as lemon pie.

77

HOLIDAY CAKE.

For this are required one-half pound of flour, one-half pound of fine granulated sugar, five eggs and a little grated lemon rind. Break the eggs into a large bowl, add the sugar, set the bowl over a saucepan of nearly boiling water, and whisk the eggs and sugar together until quite white and thick. Twenty minutes is about the time required. Add the grated lemon rind—or a few drops of essence of lemon will do as well—then stir flour into the mixture; do not beat again. Line a tin with buttered paper; over this sprinkle some sugar, then turn in the cake mixture. Bake in a quick oven one-half to three-quarters of an hour. Carefully turn out when done, set on a sieve to cool, ice with chocolate icing.

To do this put three ounces of grated chocolate and one-half wineglassful of cold water in a basin; stir till it dissolves. Put into a saucepan one-half of a pound of lump sugar and a gill of water; dissolve and boil six minutes till it is quite thick. Remove from the fire and let it stand 10 minutes, then stir the chocolate into it and spread over the cake, which may also have candied cherries and chopped pistachio nuts sprinkled over by way of decoration.

CINNAMON CAKE.

Whites of two eggs, one cup of sugar, one half cup of sweet milk, one-third cup of butter, one and one-half cups of flour, one and one-half teaspoonsful of baking powder.

Icing: Yolks of two eggs, two thirds cups of sugar, and one teaspoonfull ground cinnamon.

NEW YEAR'S CAKE.

Two cups of sugar, one and one-half cupfuls of butter, three pints of flour, three eggs, two wineglasses of milk, two of wine, two of brandy, three teaspoons of baking powder, fruit and spice to taste. Bake in deep pans according to quantity of fruit used.

CINCINNATI'S NEW WATER WORKS FROM THE KENTUCKY HIGHLAND

FRUIT GINGERBREAD.

One cup of sugar, one cup of molasses and teaspoonful of soda beaten together, three-quarter cup of butter, two eggs, one-half cup nuts, chopped fine; one-half cup seeded raisins, one-half cup currants, one cup milk, sour or buttermilk; one-half teaspoon of ginger, one-half teaspoon of cinnamon, about five cups of flour, enough to make thick as cup cake batter, perhaps a trifle thicker; add the fruit at the last. A little citron, shreded fine, is an improvement.

GINGER SNAPS.

One pint of molasses, one-half pint lard, boil together and let cool; one teaspoonful of soda, one tablespoonful of ginger, and flour enough to make dough stiff enough to roll, and cut with biscuit cutter.

SOFT GINGERBREAD.

One pint N. O. molasses, one small tea cup brown sugar, two teaspoons of soda, beat warm to a foam, three eggs well beaten, one-half pint of butter and lard mixed, one pint of sour milk, three pints of flour, two teaspoons of ginger, one of cloves and one of allspice.

GINGER COOKIES.

Three eggs, one cup butter, one pint molasses, $1\frac{1}{2}$ teaspoon soda (dissolve in warm water), a little salt, one tablespoon ginger.

SUGAR COOKIES.

Two cups sugar, one cup butter, cream together, then add one cup sour cream, one teaspoon soda, two eggs, season to taste, add flour to make a stiff dough and bake in a quick oven.

DOUGHNUTS.

Two cups sugar, four eggs, one and one-half cup rich sour cream, one teaspoonful soda, two teaspoonfuls baking powder, flour enough to make a stiff dough.

LIVE HARMONIOUSLY

A *Piano* in the home
is no longer con-
sidered a luxury
but a necessity.

A *Piano* bought
from us means
Piano content-
ment.

Pianos sold by us represent the pest and most
widely known in their respective grades. Besides
the famous EVERETT Piano, we are sole repre-
sentatives for the Hardman, John Church, Emerson,
Harvard, Steger, Harrington, Reed & Sons and the
Angelus, Cecilian and Hardman Player Pianos.

═══THE═══
CHURCH-BEINKAMP
COMPANY

CINCINNATI'S OLDEST, LARGEST
AND ONE-PRICE PIANO HOUSE

S. E. CORNER 4TH AND ELM STREETS

CHICKEN TAMALES.

The true Mexican tamales are made in the following manner: Take two pounds of corn and a handful of lime and water enough to cover; boil until the skins are loose. Wash the corn well to free from lime, and then grind it fine. Clean and joint a large chicken, and stew slowly in water in which salt has been added, until tender. Mix the ground corn with some of the stock in which the chicken has been cooked and one pound or less of lard (do not get the paste too thin); add salt to paste. Open one pound chili peppers, remove the seeds and throw them away; boil the peppers until soft. Take off the skins, press the pulp through a sieve, moistening with the chicken liquor. Add a few slices of tomatoe, three or four pieces of garlic chopped fine, and half a pound of ground chilis. Mix all with the chicken and fry a little, then boil a little; add salt; take corn husks that have been moistened in tepid water for two minutes; spread with the prepared corn meal; then put in the chicken mixture, and if you wish, boiled eggs, olives, raisins and cucumbers. Then spread another husk with the paste and lay it on the filled husk, fold and roll up as you would candy in a motto paper, tie about an inch and a half from each end and trim neatly; cook in a steamer for an hour or boil in a gallon of water, turning the top ones over when half done. This makes a dozen tamales.

CHICKEN SALAD.

Two hard boiled eggs, yolks rubbed smooth, two raw eggs, yolks well beaten, one tablespoonful of made mustard; salad oil, drop by drop until the paste thickens, one lemon (juice) or one-half cup of vinegar, two teaspoons of sugar, one teaspoon of salt, one-fourth teaspoon of pepper, or dash cayenne, two tablespoons thick, sweet cream. Make this dressing, carefully and slowly stirring in the cream just before serving. Cut the white meat of chicken into small bits, add to it as much celery, cut fine, with a silver knife; pour over it the dressing and serve. If not moist enough use some of the chicken broth.

SUPERIOR MUFFINS.

One quart of flour, one teaspoonful of salt, one tablespoonful of white sugar; rub in one heaping tablespoonful of butter and lard mixed, and one tablespoonful of Irish potato mashed very fine: pour in three well beaten eggs, a half teacup of yeast; make into a soft dough with warm water in winter and cold in summer; knead well for half an hour; let it rise where it will be milk warm in winter and cool in summer. If wanted for eight o'clock breakfast in winter, make up night before; at six o'clock in the morning make out into round balls (without kneading again) and drop into snowball molds that have been well greased; take care to grease the hands also and pass them over the tops of the muffins; set them in a warm place for two hours and then bake.

One quart New Orleans molasses, one quart buttermilk, four level teaspoons soda, two of which beat into the molasses and two into the buttermilk. Mix well; add a small handful of salt and enough Graham flour to make a batter a little thicker than for muffins. Bake in round tins about two hours. Fill tins only half full.

MUFFINS.

Separate three eggs, add to the yolks one pint milk, level teaspoonful salt, three cups flour, two heaping teaspoonfuls baking powder, one tablespoonful butter added to the milk. Bake 20 or 25 minutes.

DEVIL'S FOOD.

One and one-half cups brown sugar, one-half cup butter, one-half cup luke-warm water, one-half cup sour milk, one teaspoonful soda dissolved in one-half cup of warm water, two squares of sweet chocolate, yolks of two eggs, two cups flour; cream, butter and sugar; add grated chocolate, then eggs, sour milk. Stir in a little flour and part of water, and then the rest of flour, and finally all water.

SAGO PUDDING.

Soak three tablespoons of sago three hours in a little milk; then take one cup of sugar and the yolks of four eggs, beat them well together; have on the stove one quart of milk with the sago in it, and when hot stir in the sugar and yolks; stir constantly but do not boil, when thick turn in a baking dish, then beat the whites of the four eggs stiff and add a little powdered sugar, spread on the top and brown; flavor the custard with lemon or vanilla.

CORN PUDDING.

One can of corn, one cup of milk, one teaspoon of butter, one-quarter teaspoon of salt, two eggs. Mix well and bake in a moderate oven with the dish in a pan of cold water.

PUDDING.

Two eggs, one tablespoon of butter, two cups of fruit (canned cherries is fine for this), flour to stiffen, one teaspoon of baking powder. If not stewed fruit put in one cup of milk. Put all in a mold, steam two hours. Serve with hard sauce as follows: one-half cup of butter creamed with one cup white sugar, add one-half teaspoon lemon extract.

CHERRY PUDDING.

To a pint of sweet milk take one cup of bread crumbs; two cups of flour in which mix two teaspoons of baking powder, one teaspoon of suet or butter; two eggs. Make into a smooth batter, then stir into a pint of stoned cherries after rolling them into a part of flour. Put into a well-buttered dish and steam three hours; serve with butter and sugar or plain sauce.

RICE PUDDING WITHOUT EGGS.

Three-quarters cup of rice, one pint of milk, one pint of water or one quart of skimmed milk, sugar to sweeten, one-half grated nutmeg. four or five small pieces of butter, pinch of salt, add butter last and bake until rice is soft and slightly browned.

FIG PUDDING.

One cup chopped figs, one cup flour, one cup bread crumbs, one-half cup sugar, one-half cup suet (chopped fine), one egg, salt, two and one-half teaspoons of baking powder, spices to tast e, one ounce ir all. Grate bread and wet with milk, put all together, steam three hours. Serve with hard sauce and the following: one tablespoon of flour, one tablespoon of butter, one tablespoon of sugar, nutmeg, allspice, cinnamon to taste, pour boiling water over all.

PRUNE PUDDING.

Whites of four eggs beaten stiff; cook one-quarter pound of prunes and sweeten; strain them (be sure not to put in the juice), and stir into the whites of the eggs. Put this into a pudding dish and steam three hours. This should come out a nice light loaf. Make a boiled custard of the yolks and one pint of milk; sweeten to taste·

ENGLISH PLUM PUDDING.

One pound raisins, one pound bread crumbs, one pound currants, three eggs, one-quarter pound citron, one pound suet, one teaspoon of baking powder, two nutmegs grated, one teaspoon of salt, milk enough to moisten; cinnamon, cloves, allspice and sugar to taste. Add a little brandy. Boil in a mold for four hours.

PLAIN PLUM PUDDING.

Three cups of flour, one cup of milk, one-half cup powdered suet, one cup best molasses slightly warmed, one teaspoon soda dissolved in hot water, one-half pound raisins stoned and chopped, one-half pound currants, one egg, one teaspoon mixed cinnamon and mace, one-half teaspoon ginger, one-half teaspoon salt. Beat suet and molasses to cream; add spice, salt and two-thirds milk, stir in flour; beat hard; put in rest of milk in which the soda has been stirred. Beat up from the bottom and put in fruit well dredged with flour. Boil in buttered mold at least three hours. Eat very hot with hard sauce.

PINE APPLE SHERBET.

One pint of grated pine apple, three cups sugar, two tablespoons gelatine softened in one pint cold water, dissolved in one pint boiling water, strain ; add to the fruit the juice of two lemons. Freeze.

LEMON SHERBET.

Make a strong lemonade with six or eight lemons, rather sweet. Half freeze and turn in one pint of sweet cream. Finish freezing and let stand to ripen an hour or two.

PINEAPPLE SHERBET.

One pineapple, one and one-fourth pint of sugar, juice of two lemons, one quart of water. Grate the pineapple. Boil sugar and water together for five minutes. When cool add the juices. Strain through a cloth. Freeze. Beat the white of one egg and a tablespoon of powdered sugar. Remove the dasher, stir in this maringue, repack and stand aside until wanted.

LEMON SHERBET.

One half box Plymouth Rock gelatine, eight lemons, two pounds granulated sugar, one-half gallon boiling water. Pour one-half pint cold water on gelatine and let stand half an hour, then add one-half pint boiling water. Pour three pints boiling water on sugar and put on the stove and stir until thoroughly dissolved. Add the gelatine to syrup and when cooled add the lemon juice; strain. If gelatine is dispensed with pour two quarts boiling water over sugar; when ready to put in freezer add the well beaten white of an egg.

FRENCH LEMON SHERBET.

Make one and one-half gallons of rather acid lemonade, using twelve lemons; grate the peel of three or four, add to the lemonade and let stand twenty minutes; pour a pint of cold water over a box of gelatine, when soft pour over it one pint of boiling water; put this in the lemonade, beat whites of eight eggs with three pounds of sugar until thick as icing, have the lemonade thoroughly chilled in freezer, then add eggs and lastly one pint of whipped cream. Freeze slowly. (Delicious.)

STRAWBERRY JAM.

One heaping cup berries, one cup granulated sugar. Boil fifteen minutes.

SPICED GRAPE.

Separate the skins and pulp of Concord grapes ; one quart grape skins, one quart sugar. Cover the pulp with vinegar, boil and strain. Add the sugar and skins and two teaspoons cinnamon, one teaspoon cloves, one teaspoon allspice. Boil slowly two hours, or till skins are tender. Put in mason jars.

GOOSEBERRY FOOL.

Fruit and sugar, equal parts ; one tablespoon dried orange peel powered ; one tablespoon whole coriander seed, one and one-half teaspoons cloves,one and one-half teaspoons cassia buds or cinnamon. Cook till thick as ordinary preserves, the add one-half cup pure cider vinegar. It will keep without canning.

ORANGE JELLY AND BASKETS,

One-half box gelatine, one-half cup cold water, one cup boiling water, juice of one lemon, one cup sugar, one pint orange juice. Soak the gelatine in the cold water until soft, then add the boiling water, lemon juice, sugar and orange juice. Stir till the sugar is dissolved and strain. The oranges can be cut in half, and when the inside is removed, use for the jelly and a spoonful of whipped cream put on each ; or baskets can be made by leaving half the peel whole, and a strip half an inch wide for the handle.

CORN BREAD.

One pint sour milk, one teaspoon soda dissolved in milk ; one egg, ½ teacup sugar, one teaspoon salt, corn meal sufficient to make a thick batter. Bake in hot oven thirty minutes.

QUINCE HONEY.

Grate four quinces and three apples ; add one pint of water and three and one-half pounds of sugar. Boil twenty minutes.

ORANGE SHORTCAKE.

Peel five or six oranges, chop very fine, removing the seeds. Add a teacup of powdered sugar. Making a good baking powder shortcake, divide, put a layer of the filling into one half; sweeten if desired, cover and spread the orange filling over the top. Put a tablespoonful of whipped cream over each section when served.

SWEETBREAD CROQUETTES.

Mix together one-half cup of warm boiled rice, one-half can of mushrooms, chopped fine and one sweetbread which has been parboiled and chopped fine; season to taste with salt and pepper and moisten with a hot thick cream sauce until it is soft enough to be handled. When cool, shape, roll in fine bread crumbs, then slip into beaten egg and again in bread crumbs and fry in hot fat. Calf's brain may be parboiled, mixed with sweetbreads and used in the same way for croquettes.

APPLE MARINGUES.

Pare, slice, stew and sweeten to taste ripe, juicy apples; mash smoothly and season with nutmeg or lemon peel. Line a deep plate with an under-crust, fill it nearly to the top with the prepared apples and bake until the crust is done. Beat the whites of three fresh eggs to a stiff froth, then beat in three tablespoonfuls of sugar, spread over the pie and return to a rather cool oven to give the top a dainty brown color. The pie may be eaten either warm or cold. Dried peaches or fruit of any kind may be substituted for the apples.

ALMOND WAFERS.

Cream one-half cup of butter; add slowly one cup of powdered sugar and one-half cup of milk drop by drop. Then stir in one and seven-eights cups of bread flour and one-half teaspoonful almond extract. Spread this mixture out in a thin sheet on the bottom of an inverted dripping pan that has been buttered. Mark in squares, sprinkle with almonds, blanched and chopped, and bake in a moderate oven five minutes.

VIEW OF EASTERN SECTION OF CINCINNATI—ROOKWOOD POTTERY ON THE BROW OF HILL TO LEFT

LIGHT ROLLS.

One pint milk, one pint water, one cake of yeast, one tablespoon sugar, teaspoon salt, tablespoon lard. Put the lard in the milk and let it come to a boil; then cool with the water. Beat the batter well before putting in the yeast. Let it rise. Then make into rolls about two hours before baking.

DEVIL'S FOOD.

Two large cups light brown sugar, one-half cup butter, two eggs, one-third cup grated chocolate, one-third cup sour milk, one-half cup boiling water, three cups flour, one teaspoonful of soda, one-half cup raisins, one-half cup nuts, and citron if desired. Pour part of boiling water over chocolate, the rest over soda.

DEVIL'S FOOD

Two cups brown sugar, one-half cup butter, two eggs, (not beaten) one-half cake Baker's chocolate dissolved in one-half cup boiling water, one level teaspoonful soda dissolved in one-half cup sour milk, three cups flour. Filling: one cup sweet milk; two cups brown sugar and small piece of butter; boil until strings, and stir until cold.

RIBBON CAKE.

Two cups of sugar, two-thirds cup of butter, one cup sweet milk, three cups flour, three eggs, one teaspoon soda, salt and essence of lemon or almond. Put one half of this in two oblong pans, and to the remainder add one tablespoon molasses, one large cup raisins, chopped and stoned, one-quarter pound citron, sliced, one teaspoon cinnamon, one-half teaspoon each of cloves and allspice, one table-spoon flour and a little grated nutmeg. Bake in two sheets. Put the sheets together alternately, when warm, with cranberry or any tart jelly between.

WAFFLES.

Two eggs, one tablespoonful of lard and one tablespoonful of butter melted, one pint of milk and water, pinch of salt, two tea-spoonfuls of baking powder with flour enough to make the batter stiff; add the whites of the eggs, well beaten, last.

The Most Economical Refrigerator

Is not one that is cheapest in first cost. It is the one that *keeps things fresh* with the least ice.

An "ice-box" that costs $10.00 will be much more expensive than a McCRAY REFRIGERATOR that costs three times as much, because the McCray will will soon pay for itself in saving on ice and provisions; but the $10.00 "ice-box" being an "ice-eater" is a constant expense.

McCRAY
REFRIGERATORS
(*Keep things fresh*)

They are so strongly built that they will last indefinitely, like the good furniture that is handed down from generation to generation.

Tainted butter and milk that is not quite fresh do not enhance domestic bliss.

We respectfully suggest, therefore, that you come in and see our McCray Refrigerators before purchasing.

McCray Refrigerator Co.
CHARLES R. DUNTON, MANAGER.

236 MAIN STREET, - - CINCINNATI, O.

FACTORY AT KENDALLVILLE, IND.

STRAWBERRY PRESERVE.

To every one pint fruit add one pint sugar and one-fourth pint water. Put water and sugar on to boil till it will gather in water (three or four minutes) : then put in the berries and let boil twenty minutes, take off and pour into an earthen crock and let stand until next day. Then drain off syrup and cook till it will jelly, then add fruit and boil ten minutes ; put away in jelly glasses.

PINE APPLE SNOW.

Soak one cup of flake tapioca in one-half pint of water two hours; to this add one cup sugar, little salt, one pint water, then boil till clear; add juice of one can of pineapple and then the stiff whites of three eggs, then the pineapple cut in small pieces; mix well; serve with custard. Custard: three yolks, one cup sugar, vanilla to taste, one pint milk.

DOUGHNUTS.

To two well beaten eggs, add one cup of sugar, one-half teaspoon salt; put one teaspoon soda in one cup buttermilk, and add to the eggs and sugar; beat all together, then add two tablespoonsful of hot lard from the kettle; stir in flour enough to make a soft dough.

COTTAGE PUDDING.

One egg, two teaspoons of baking powder, two cups flour, one cup of sugar, one cup of milk, two tablespoons of butter, juice of one lemon, bake as cake and serve with sauce.

FRUIT PUFFS.

Beat one egg, add one cup of milk; slowly pour this on two cups of flour sifted with two teaspoonfuls of baking powder and one half teaspoonful salt. Add one teaspoonful of butter, melted, sprinkle one pint of fruit with one fourth cup of flour and add the first mixture gently to it. Pour into six greased cups and steam for 15 minutes, closely covered.

=*Fruitrye*=

A FINE FOOD DRINK

The concentrated strength of Malt and Fruits. A liquid food that is rich with nourishing Malt. It will rebuild your wasted tissues, steady your tired worn out nerves and give you sweet refreshing sleep. Builds you up so fast it will open your eyes.

THIS BEAUTIFUL TEASPOON IS FOR YOU!

With every bottle of *Fruitrye,* enclosed in the carton, you will find a full sized silver-plated Teaspoon, exclusive in design, a rich dull gray in the very latest French finish.

BUY A BOTTLE TODAY!

—AT—

Dow's DRUGSTORES

7th & Race
6th & Walnut
4th & Main

ICE CREAM.

To two quarts of rich cream crush and dissolve one pound of peppermint candy.

VEAL LOAF.

Three pounds of veal, three eggs, one-fourth cup of butter, one teaspoon of black pepper, two teaspoons of salt, three tablespoons of cream, one teaspoon of onion juice, one-half teaspoon of allspice, one teaspoon of summer savory, one-half cup of bread or cracker crumbs. Bake slowly in a moderate oven for three hours.

FILIPINO LOAF.

One and one-half pounds of lean beef, half pound of fresh pork, one onion and two peppers. Chop fine, add one cup of bread crumbs; a high seasoning of salt and pepper. Make into loaf; lay slices of bacon on top; pour over a can of tomatoes. Bake one and one-half hours.

MEAT LOAF.

Three pounds of beef (ground or chopped fine), one cup cracker crumbs, one cup water, two eggs beaten well, one teaspoon pepper three of salt. Mix well together, place in a covered baking pan, press down, set pan into larger one containing a little water and bake in a hot oven one and a half hours. Slice when cold and serve.

FRENCH PICKLES.

One peck of green tomatoes sliced, six large onions; mix these and throw over them one cup (tea) salt and let stand over night. Drain thoroughly and boil in one quart of vinegar and two quarts of water for fifteen or twenty minutes. Then throw this away and take four quarts fresh vinegar, two pounds brown sugar, one-fourth pound white mustard seed, two tablespoons ground allspice, two of cinnamon, two of cloves, two of ginger, two of ground mustard. Boil all together with the vinegar and tomatoes for fifteen minutes. Seal in mason jars.

MARGUERITES.

Get the long thin wafers and spread thickly with the beaten whites of two eggs. Thicken with pulverized sugar, one-half pound chopped almonds or peanuts. Stir all into another white of an egg, beaten light without sugar. Brown a few minutes in the oven. Serve with ice cream or gelatine.

QUINCE HONEY.

Take one pound of granulated sugar to each large quince, or two pounds to three small ones. Use as many quinces and sugar in this proportion as you like. Grate the quinces. Make rich syrup of the sugar, but not quite to the hairing point; then put in the grated quinces, boil ten minutes and seal while hot.

PEACH MOUSE.

Peel and slice enough peaches to make one pint; one-half pint sugar, one pint whipped cream.

CUCUMBER CATSUP.

Three dozen cucumbers, one and one-half dozen onions, one cup of salt; mix well drain in a sieve over night. Add five cents worth of white mustard seed, five cents worth of celery seed. Season with black pepper, add a little horse radish and cover with vinegar.

TOMATO CATSUP.

One-half bushel ripe tomatoes, four ounces allspice, one ounce cloves, one-fourth ounce cayenne pepper, one pint fine salt, one-half gallon cider vinegar, one ounce gum tragacanth, two ounces of ginger root. Boil tomatoes without peeling and rub through colander. Then put in the preserving kettle with all the ingredients except the gum and vinegar and boil five hours. (Split the ginger root so the strength will boil out.) When you strain the tomatoes, save out a pint of the juice and put the gum to soak in, stirring occasionally that it may dissolve before putting it into the kettle. Add the vinegar and gum just before it is done, and bring to a boil, after which strain through a sieve and bottle. *Use whole spices.*

HENRY PROBASCO

One Of Cincinnati's Benefactors.

CHERRY COBLER.

Take two quarts of cherries, stone and sweeten them. Then put in a pan with a little flour sprinkled over them ; put a cup in the center with a weight on it, then turn the following cake over the cherries. Cake : one-half cup butter, one cup sugar, two eggs, one cup milk and three cups flour, one teaspoon baking powder. Serve with a hot dip.

MINCED HALIBUT.

Take a thick, fresh halibut steak, put in boiling water and cook until tender—about one-half an hour, then pick free of the bones, making it very fine. Chop fine one small onion and put in a skillet with one pint of milk and two heaping tablespoons of butter ; let it boil a little and then add three eggs and one tablespoon of flour (mixed in a little milk) and a small amount of chopped parsley ; when it thickens pour over the minced halibut, mix well, then put in oyster shells and sprinkle over them some nice browned and rolled bread crumbs when ready to serve, warm a few moments ; salt and pepper the dressing while cooking to taste.

FINE CODFISH BALLS.

Take a package of salt codfish, or a nice thick piece, and wash well in tepid water. Soak over night, then in the morning pick in small bits, have enough to fill a pint ; then peel enough potatoes and cut in pieces to make a pint ; cook them together in boiling water about twenty minutes until the potatoes are soft, but not watery. Drain off the water and shake well over the fire to make light and dry ; whip well, (use a fork or wire beater) put in a teaspoon of butter and pepper to taste ; add salt if needed, then whip in a well beaten egg. Cook same as doughnuts. Be sure your lard is very hot. Dip a tablespoon into the hot lard, then into the mixture and let the spoon shape it—it will come out egg shaped. Don't cook but four or five balls at a time ; they should not touch.

POTTER'S
18-20-22-24 W. FIFTH ST.,
CINCINNATI, OHIO

THE GREAT HOME SHOE STORE OF
THE QUEEN CITY, WE BEGAN FITTING
CINCINNATI PEOPLE IN SHOES IN
1866 AND SLOWLY, BUT SURELY, OUR
BUSINESS HAS GROWN TO BE THE

LARGEST IN THE MIDDLE WEST.

ISN'T THIS THE BEST EVIDENCE THAT
OUR CUSTOMERS HAVE BEEN WELL
TREATED ?

CLAM OR FISH CHOWDER.

NICE FOR LUNCHEON.—Cut six slices pickled pork into small pieces and put in the bottom of the kettle, let in cook slowly till fat is all out and the meat is brown. Slice four medium sized onions into this and let them get a rich brown ; add eight potatoes, peeled and sliced quite thin, and cover with boiling water. If you are making *fish* chowder, add two pounds of sliced fresh cod, or any good solid fish and boil this until the fish and potatoes are done—about half an hour. Add salt and pepper to taste before boiling.

If making *clam* chowder add one dozen nice clams cut fine, or one can of good clams, put in all the juice after the potatoes are done and just let it come to a boil. Lastly, add one quart milk and let come to a boil. Do not boil or the milk will curdle. Serve with crackers.

CLAM CHOWDER.

Take a peck of clams and steam them and chop them up fine, saving the liquor; take a half pound of salt pork, cutting up in pieces the size of dice and fry brown until all the grease is out of it; take six onions, medium size, and cut in pieces the size of the pork; take two quarts of potatoes and cut up the same size, 10 large tomatoes and slice them and a pound of oyster crackers. Take a kettle and put a layer of pork, then a layer of clam, one of onions, one of potatoes, tomatoes, then one of crackers; repeat until all the ingredients are used, season to taste, then pour the clam liquor over them and close tight and set on the fire, and let simmer for an hour and a half.

HARD SAUCE.

Cream one-half cupful pulverized sugar and one tablespoon of butter, flavor with lemon or nutmeg. Beat stiff the white of an egg, stir in thoroughly the sugar and butter; shape and set in a cool place until ready for use.

WARM BREAD.

Dough after it has become once sufficiently raised and perfectly light, cannot afterwards be injured by setting aside in any cold place where it cannot *freeze;* therefore, biscuits, rolls, etc., can be made late the day before wanted for breakfast. Prepare them ready for baking by molding them out late in the evening; lay them a little apart on buttered tins; cover the tins with a cloth, then fold around that a newspaper, so as to exclude the air, as that has a tendency to cause the crust to be hard and thick when baked. The best place in summer is to place them in the ice-box, then all you have to do in the morning (an hour before breakfast time, and while the oven is heating) is to bring them from the ice-box, take off the cloth and warm it, and place it over them again; then set the tins in a warm place near the fire. This will give them time to rise and bake when needed. If these directions are followed rightly, you will find it makes no difference with their lightness and goodness, and you can always be sure of warm raised biscuits for breakfast in one hour's time.

Stale rolls may be made light and flakey by dipping for a moment in cold water, and placing immediately in a very hot oven to be made crisp and hot.

EGG MUFFINS.

One quart of flour, sifted twice; twice eggs, the whites and yolks beaten separately, three teacups of sweet milk, a teaspoonful of salt, a tablespoonful of sugar, a large tablespoonful of lard or butter and two heaping teaspoonfuls of baking powder. Sift together flour, sugar, salt and baking powder; rub in the lard cold, add the beaten eggs and milk; mix quickly into a smooth batter, a little firmer than for griddle-cakes. Grease well some muffins-pans and fill them two-thirds full. Bake in a hot oven fifteen or twenty minutes. These made of cream, omitting the butter, are excellent.

HOUSEHOLD HINT No. 1

Do not overlook the importance of ice in the home.

There is scarcely a commodity in your domestic arrangements which brings equal results.

In health or sickness, ice has become one of the prime necessities of life.

We have splendid facilities for making deliveries at a time suitable to your requirements.

Our wagons handle nothing but the highest grade of absolutely pure ice.

A TRIAL CONVINCES.

The Ice Delivery Company

Offices: N. W. Cor, Race & Canal Sts,
TELEPHONE CANAL 1772   CINCINNATI, O.

"ICE WHEN YOU WANT IT"

WHEAT GRIDDLE CAKES.

Three cups of flour, one teaspoonful of salt, three teaspoonfuls of baking powder sifted together; beat three eggs and add to three cupfuls of sweet milk, also a tablespoonful of melted butter; mix all into a smooth batter, as thick as will run in a stream from the lips of a pitcher. Bake on a well-greased, hot griddle, a nice light brown. Very good.

WAFFLES.

Take a quart of flour and wet it with a little sweet milk that has been boiled and cooled, then stir in enough of the milk to form a thick batter. Add a teaspoonful of salt, and yeast to raise it. When light add two well-beaten eggs, heat your waffle iron, grease it well and fill it with the batter. Two or three minutes will suffice to bake on one side; then turn the iron over, and when brown on both sides the cake is done. Serve immediately.

PLAIN GRAHAM GEMS.

Two cupfuls of the best Graham meal, two of water, fresh and cold, or milk and water, and a little salt. Stir briskly for a minute or two. Have the gem pan, hot and well greased, on the top of the stove while pouring in the batter. Then place in a very hot oven and bake forty minutes. It is best to check the heat a little when they are nearly done. As the best prepared gems may be spoiled if the heat is not sufficient, care and judgement must be used in order to secure this most healthful as well as delicious bread.

PLAIN MUFFINS.

One egg well beaten, a tablespoonful of butter, and a tablespoonful of sugar, with a teaspoonful of salt, all beaten until very light. One cup of milk, three of sifted flour and three teaspoonfuls of baking powder. One-half graham and one-half rye meal may be used instead of wheat flour, or two cups of corn meal and one of flour.

Drop on well-greased patty-pan and bake twenty minutes in a rather quick oven, or bake on a griddle in muffin-rings.

APPLE FRITTERS.

Make a batter in the proportion of one cup sweet milk to two cups flour, a heaping teaspoonful of baking powder, two eggs beaten separately, one tablespoonful of sugar and a teaspoon of salt; heat the milk a little more than milk-warm, add it slowly to the beaten yolks and sugar; then add flour and whites of eggs; stir all together and throw in thin slices of good sour apples, dipping the batter up over them; drop into boiling hot lard in large spoonfuls with pieces of apple in each, and fry to a light brown.   Serve with maple syrup, or a nice syrup made with clarified sugar.

Bananas, peaches, sliced oranges and other fruits can be used in the same batter.

CORN MEAL GRIDDLE CAKES.

Stir into one quart of boiling milk three cups of corn meal; after it cools add one cup of white flour, a teaspoonful of salt and three tablespoonfuls of home-made yeast. Mix this over night.   In the morning add one tablespoonful of melted butter or lard, two beaten eggs and a teaspoonful of soda dissolved in a little water.

This batter should stand a few minutes, after adding the butter and soda, that it should have time to rise a little; in the meantime the griddle could be heating.   Take a small stick like a good-sized skewer, wind a bit of cloth around the end of it, fasten it by winding a piece of thread around that and tying it firm.   Melt together a tablespoonful of butter and lard.   Grease the griddle with this. Between each batch of cakes, wipe the griddle off with a clean paper or cloth and grease afresh.   Put the cakes on by spoonfuls, or pour them carefully from a pitcher, trying to get them as near the same size as possible.   As soon as they begin to bubble all over turn them, and cook on the other side till they stop puffing.   The second lot always cooks better than the first, as the griddle becomes evenly heated.

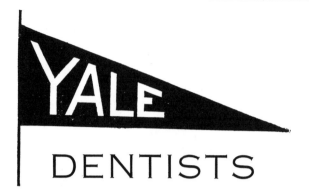

DENTISTS

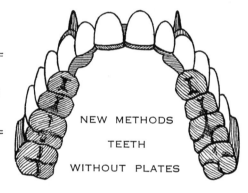

BUCKWHEAT CAKES.

Half a pint of buckwheat flour, a quarter of a pint of corn meal, a quarter of a pint of wheat flour, a little salt, two eggs beaten very light, one quart of new milk (made a little warm and mixed with the eggs before the flour is put in), one tablespoonful of butter or sweet lard, two large tablespoonfuls of yeast. Set it to rise at night for the morning. If in the least sour, stir in before baking just enough soda to correct the acidity.

BUCKWHEAT CAKES.

Take a small crock or large earthen pitcher, put into it a quart of warm water or half water and milk, one heaping teaspoonful of salt; then stir in as much buckwheat flour as will thicken it to rather a stiff batter; lastly, add half a cup of yeast; make it smooth, cover it up warm to rise over night; in the morning add a small, level teaspoonful of soda dissolved in a little warm water; this will remove any sour taste, if any, and increase the lightness.

Not a few object to eating buckwheat, as its tendency is to thicken the blood, and also to produce constipation; this can be remedied by making the batter one-third corn meal and two-thirds buckwheat, which makes the cakes equally as good. Many prefer them in this way.

FRENCH ROLLS.

Three cups of sweet milk, one cup of butter and lard, mixed in equal proportions, one-half cup of good yeast, or half a cake of compressed yeast, and a teaspoonful of salt. Add flour enough to make a stiff dough. Let it rise over night; in the morning, add two well-beaten eggs; knead thoroughly and let it rise again. With the hands, make it into balls as large as an egg; then roll between the hands to make *long rolls* (about three inches). Place close together in even rows on well-buttered pans. Cover and let them rise again, then bake in a quick oven to a delicate brown.

YEAST RUSKS.

In one large coffeecup of warm milk dissolve half a cake of compressed yeast, or three tablespoonfuls of home-made yeast; to this add three well-beaten eggs, a small cup of sugar and a teaspoonful of salt; beat these together. Use flour enough to make a smooth, light dough, let it stand until very light, then knead it in the form of biscuits; place them on buttered tins and let them rise until they are almost up to the edge of the tins; pierce the top of each one and bake in a quick oven. Glaze the top of each with sugar and milk, or the white of an egg, before baking. Some add dried currants, well-washed and dried in the oven.

BEATEN BISCUIT.

Two quarts of sifted flour, a teaspoonful of salt, a tablespoonful of sweet lard, one egg; make up with half a pint of milk, or if milk is not to be had, plain water will answer; beat well until the dough blisters and cracks; pull off a two-inch square of the dough; roll it into a ball with the hand; flatten, stick with a fork, and bake in a quick oven.

It is not beating hard that makes the biscuit nice, but the regularity of the motion.

SARAH LYNN.

Warm one-half cupful of butter in a pint of milk; add a teaspoonful of salt, a tablespoonful of sugar, and seven cupfuls of *sifted* flour; beat thoroughly and when the mixture is blood warm, add four beaten eggs and last of all, half a cup of good lively yeast. Beat hard until the batter breaks in blisters. Set it to rise over night. In the morning, dissolve half a teaspoonful of soda, stir it into the batter and turn into a well-buttered, shallow dish to rise again about fifteen or twenty minutes. Bake about fifteen to twenty minutes.

The cake should be torn apart, not cut; cutting with a knife makes warm bread heavy. Bake a light brown.

BEFORE PURCHASING ELSEWHERE
VISIT THE EXCLUSIVE SHOP

IN

TRUNKS, SUIT CASES, TRAVELING BAGS

AND IN FACT EVERYTHING THAT IS MADE OF

LEATHER

WE HAVE THE BEST AND MOST COMPLETE LINE AT

POPULAR PRICES

LONG'S TRUNK STORE
438 RACE STREET,

CINCINNATI, OHIO

GIBSON HOUSE ROLLS.

One pint of milk, boiled and cooled, a piece of butter the size of an egg, one-half cupful of fresh yeast, one tablespoonful of sugar, one pinch of salt, and two quarts of sifted flour.

Melt the butter in the warm milk, then add the sugar, salt and flour, and let it rise over night. Mix rather soft. In the morning, add to this half of a teaspoonful of soda dissolved in a spoonful of water. Mix in enough flour to make the same stiffness as any biscuit dough; roll out not more than a quarter of an inch thick. Cut with a large round cutter; spread soft butter over the tops and fold one-half over the other by doubling it. Place them apart so that there will be room to rise. Cover and place them near the fire for fifteen or twenty minutes before baking. Bake in rather a quick oven.

HOT BUNS.

Three cups of milk, one cup of yeast, or one cake of compressed yeast dissolved in a cup of tepid water, and flour enough to make a thick batter; set this as a sponge over night. In the morning add half a cup of melted butter, one cup of sugar, half a nutmeg grated, one teaspoonful of salt, half a teaspoonful of soda, and flour enough to roll out like biscuit, knead well and set to rise for five hours. Roll the dough half an inch thick; cut in round cakes and lay in rows in a buttered baking-pan, and let the cakes stand half an hour, or until light then put them in the oven, having first made a deep cross on each with a knife. Bake a light brown and brush over with white of egg beaten stiff with powdered sugar.

SODA BISCUIT.

One quart of sifted flour, one teaspoonful of soda, two teaspoonfuls of cream of tartar, one teaspoonful of salt; mix thoroughly, and rub in two tablespoonfuls of butter and wet with one pint of sweet milk. Bake in a quick over.

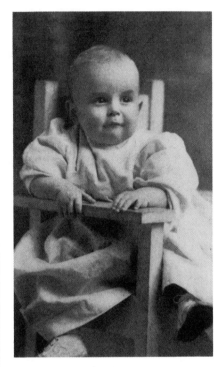

THE *newly wed, of course, had all the comforts of home with their parents, but were never one-tenth as happy as when installed in a home of their own.*

There are little children to whom "Father" is but a memory and "Mother" but a dream. **THE CHILDREN'S HOME on Ninth Street, Cincinnati,** *furnishes to such both a home with foster parents and also a preparation for a home of their own when they shall be grown up.*

Rejoice, oh young husband and wife, in your privilege! But also please remember the little ones in their homelessness and help **THE CHILDREN'S HOME** *to make their lives good and to save them from the days, which may be many, of darkness and evil.*

SOUR MILK BISCUIT.

Rub into a quart of sifted flour a piece of butter the size of an egg, one teaspoonful of salt; stir into this a pint of sour milk, dissolve one teaspoonful of soda and stir into the milk just as you add it to the flour; knead it up quickly, roll it out nearly half an inch thick and cut out with a biscuit-cutter; bake immediately in a quick oven.

Very nice biscuit may be made with sour cream without the butter by the same process.

CORN MEAL FRITTERS.

One pint of sour milk, one teaspoonful of salt, three eggs, one tablespoonful of molasses or sugar, one handful of flour, and corn meal enough to make a stiff batter; lastly, stir in a small teaspoonful of soda, dissolve in a little warm water.

This recipe is very nice made of rye flour.

CREAM TARTS.

Make a rich, brittle crust, with which cover your patty-pans, smoothing off the edges nicely and bake well. While these "shells" are cooling, take one teacupful (more or less according to the number of tarts you want) of perfectly sweet and fresh cream, skimmed free of milk; put this into a large bowl or other deep dish, and with your egg-beater whip it to a thick, stiff froth; add a heaping tablespoonful of fine white sugar, with a teaspoonful (a small one) of lemon or vanilla. Fill the cold shells with this and set in a cool place till tea is ready.

CRANBERRY TART PIE.

After having washed and picked over the berries, stew them well .n a little water, just enough to cover them; when they burst open and become soft, sweeten them with plenty of sugar, mash them smooth (some prefer them not mashed); line your pie-plates with thin puff paste, fill them and lay strips of paste across the top. Bake in a moderate oven. Or you may rub them through a colander to free them from the skins.

HOW TO MAKE A PIE.

After making the crust, take a portion of it, roll it out and fit it to a buttered pie-plate by cutting it off evenly around the edge; gather up the scraps left from cutting and make into another sheet for the top crust; roll it a little thinner than the under crust; lap one-half over the other and cut three or four slits about a quarter of an inch from the folded edge (this prevents the steam from escaping through the rim of the pie, and causing the juices to run out from the edges). Now fill your pie-plate with your prepared filling, wet the top edge of the rim, lay the upper crust across the center of the pie, turn back the half that is lapped over, seal the two edges together by slightly pressing down with your thumb, then notch evenly and regularly with a three-tined fork, dipping occasionly in flour to prevent sticking. Bake in a rather quick oven a light brown, and until the filling boils up through the slits in the upper crust.

To prevent the juice soaking through into the crust, making it soggy, wet the under crust with the white of an egg, just before you put in the pie mixture. If the top of the pie is brushed over with the egg, it gives it a beautiful glaze.

PATTIES, OR SHELLS FOR TARTS.

Roll out a nice puff paste thin; cut out with a glass or cooky-cutter and with a wine-glass or smaller cutter, cut out the center of two out of three; lay the rings thus made on the third, and bake at once. May be used for veal or oyster patties, or filled with jelly, jam or preserves, as tarts. Or shells may be made by lining patty-pans with paste. If the paste is light, the shell will be fine. Filled with jelly and covered with maringue (tablespoonful of sugar to the white of one egg) and browned in oven, they are very nice to serve for tea.

If the cutters are dipped in *hot water*, the edges of the tartlets will rise much higher and smoother when baking.

Leonard
Cleanable Refrigerators
Are Easy to Clean

Ready access to all parts of the Leonard Cleanable Refrigerator is a strong factor in its popularity. Shelves and drain pipe are instantly removable. It is then but the work of a minute to clean the smooth, white walls of porcelain, with no obstructions of any kind to hinder. A stream of water sent through the drain pipe quickly empties that of any dirt or obstructions, drain pipe and shelves can be set back in a twinkling—and it's just as easy as it sounds. There is no refrigerator as good as the Leonard Cleanable and none you will like better after you see it. Twelve walls to save the ice. Come in and let us show you it's value.

LOUIS MARX & BROS.
COVINGTON, KY.   NEWPORT, KY.

CUSTARD PIE.

Beat together until very light the yolks of four eggs and four tablespoonfuls of sugar, flavor with nutmeg or vanilla; then add the four beaten whites, a pinch of salt and, lastly, a quart of sweet milk; mix well and pour into tins lined with paste. Bake until firm.

CHERRY PIE.

Line your pie plate with good crust, fill half full with ripe cherries, sprinkle over them about a cupful of sugar, a teaspoonful of sifted flour, dot a few bits of butter over that. Now fill the crust full to the top. Cover with the upper crust and bake.

This is one of the best of pies, if made correctly, and the cherries in any case should be stoned.

RHUBARB PIE.

Cut the large stocks off where the leaves commence, strip off the outskin, then cut the stalks in pieces half an inch long; line a pie dish with paste rolled rather thicker than a dollar piece, put a layer of the rhubarb nearly an inch deep; to a quart bowl of cut rhubarb put a large teacupful of sugar; strew it over with a saltspoonful of salt and a little nutmeg grated; shake over a little flour; cover with a rich pie crust, cut a slit in the centre, trim off the edge with a sharp knife and bake in a quick oven until the pie loosens from the dish. Rhubarb pies made in this way are altogether superior to those made of the fruit stewed.

PEACH PIE.

Peel, stone and slice the peaches. Line a pie-plate with crust and lay in your fruit, sprinkling sugar liberally over them in proportion to their sweetness. Allow three peach kernels chopped fine to each pie; pour in a very little water and bake with an upper crust, or with cross-bars of paste across the top.

MINCE PIES.

Four pounds of lean boiled beef chopped fine, twice as much of chopped green tart apples, one pound of chopped suet, three pounds of raisins, seeded, two pounds of currants picked over, washed and dried, half a pound of citron, cut up fine, one pound of brown sugar, one quart of cooking molasses, two quarts of sweet cider, one pint of boiled cider, one tablespoonful of salt, one tablespoonful of pepper, one tablespoonful of mace, one tablespoonful of allspice and four tablespoonfuls of cinnamon, two grated nutmegs, one tablespoonful of cloves; mix thoroughly and warm it on the range until heated through. Remove from the fire and when nearly cool, stir in a pint of good brandy and one pint of Madeira wine. Put into a crock, cover it tightly and set it in a cold place where it will not freeze, but keep perfectly cold. Will keep good all winter.

APPLE TARTS.

Pare, quarter, core and boil in half a cupful of water, until quite soft, ten large, tart apples; beat until very smooth and add the yolks of six eggs, or three whole ones, the juice and grated outside rind of two lemons, half a cup of butter, one and a half of sugar (or more, if not sufficiently sweet); beat all thoroughly, line patty-pans with a puff paste and fill; bake five minutes in a hot oven.

Meringue:—If desired very nice, cover them when removed from the oven with the meringue made of the whites of three eggs remaining. mixed with three tablespoonfuls sugar; return to the oven and delicately brown.

CRANBERRY PIE.

Take fine, sound, ripe cranberries and with a sharp knife split each one until you have a heaping coffeecupful; put them in a vegetable dish or basin; put over them one cupful of white sugar, half a cup of water, a tablespoonful of sifted flour; stir it all together and put into your crust. You will find this the true way of making a cranberry pie.

128

GOOSEBERRY PIE.

Can be made the same as "Cranberry Tart Pie," or an upper crust can be put on before baking. Serve with boiled custard or a pitcher of good sweet cream

PUMPKIN PIE.

For three pies: One quart of milk, three cupfuls of boiled and strained pumpkin. one and one-half cupfuls of sugar, one-half cupful of molasses, the yolks and whites of four eggs beaten separately, a little salt, one tablespoonful each of ginger and cinnamon. Beat all together and bake with an under crust.

Boston marrow or Hubbard squash may be substituted for pumpkin and are much preferred by many, possessing a less strong flavr.

FLOATING ISLANDS.

Beat the yolks of five eggs and the whites of two very light, sweeten with five tablespoonfuls of sugar and flavor to taste; stir them into a quart of scalded milk and cook it until it thickens. When cool pour it into a glass dish. Now whip the whites of the three remaining eggs to a stiff froth, adding three tablespoonfuls of sugar and a little flavoring. Pour this froth over a shallow dish of boiling water; the steam passing through it cooks it; when sufficiently cooked, take a tablespoon and drop spoonfuls of this over the top of the custard, far enough apart so that the "little white islands" will not touch each other. By dropping a teaspoonful of bright jelly on the top or center of each island, is produced a pleasing effect; also by filling wine-glasses and arranging them around a standard adds much to the appearance of the table.

TAPIOCA BLANC MANGE.

Half a pound of tapioca soaked an hour in one pint of milk and boiled until tender; add a pinch of salt, sweeten to taste and put into a mold; when cold turn it out and serve with strawberry or raspberry jam around it and a little cream. Flavor with lemon or vanilla.

CUP CUSTARD.

Six eggs, half a cupful of sugar, one quart of new milk. Beat the eggs and the sugar and milk, and any extract or flavoring you like. Fill your custard cups, sift a little nutmeg or cinnamon over the tops, set them in a moderate oven in a shallow pan half filled with hot water. In about twenty minutes try them with the handle of a teaspoon to see if they are firm. Judgment and great care are needed to attain skill in baking custard, for if left in the oven a minute too long, or if the fire is too hot, the milk will certainly whey.

WHIPPED CREAM.

To the whites of three eggs, beaten to a stiff froth, add a pint of thick sweet cream (previously set where it is very cold) and four tablespoonfuls of sweet wine, with three of fine white sugar and a teaspoonful of the extract of lemon or vanilla. Mix all the ingredients together on a broad platter or pan and whip it to a standing froth; as the froth rises, take it off lightly with a spoon and lay it on an inverted sieve with a dish under it to catch what will drain through; and what drains through can be beaten over again.

Serve in a glass dish with jelly or jam and sliced sponge cake. This should be whipped in a cool place and set in the ice box.

BANANA CREAM.

After peeling the bananas, mash them with an iron or wooden spoon; allow equal quantities of bananas and sweet cream; to one quart of the mixture, allow one-quarter of a pound of sugar. Beat them all together until the cream is light.

TAPIOCA CREAM CUSTARD.

Soak three heaping tablespoonfuls of tapioca in a teacupful of water over night. Place over the fire a quart of milk; let it come to a boil, then stir in the tapioca, a good pinch of salt, stir until it thickens; then add a cupful of sugar and the beaten yolks of three eggs. Stir it quickly and pour it into a dish and stir gently into the mixture the whites beaten stiff, the flavoring and set it on ice, or in an ice chest.

EAST END CINCINNATI FROM EDEN PARK, ISLAND QUEEN IN MID STREAM

GREEN APPLE PIE.

Peel, core and slice tart apples enough for a pie; sprinkle over about three tablespoonfuls of sugar, a teaspoonful of cinnamon, a small level tablespoonful of sifted flour, two tablespoonfuls of water, a few bits of butter, stir all together with a spoon; put it into a pie-tin lined with pie paste; cover with a top crust and bake about forty minutes. The result will be a delicious, juicy pie.

LEMON PIE.

Take a deep dish, grate into it the outside of the rind of two lemons; add to that a cup and a half of white sugar, two heaping tablespoonfuls of unsifted flour, or one of cornstarch; stir it well together, then add the yolks of three well-beaten eggs, beat this thoroughly, then add the juice of the lemons, two cups of water and a piece of butter the size of a walnut. Set this on the fire in another dish containing boiling water and cook it until it thickens, and will dip up on the spoon like cold honey. Remove it from the fire, and when cooled, pour it into a deep pie-tin, lined with pastry; bake and when done, have ready the whites, beaten stiff, with three small tablespoonfuls of sugar. Spread this over the top and return to the oven to set and brown slightly. This makes a deep large sized pie, and very superior.

PLAIN PIE CRUST.

Two and a half cupfuls of sifted flour, one cupful of shortening, half butter and half lard cold, a pinch of salt, a heaping teaspoonful of baking powder sifted through the flour. Rub thoroughly the shortening into the flour. Mix together with a half a teacupful of *cold* water, or enough to form a rather stiff dough; mix as little as possible, just enough to get it into shape to roll out; it must be handled very lightly. This rule is for two pies.

When you have a little pie crust left do not throw it away; roll it thin, cut it in small squares and bake. Just before tea put a spoonful of raspberry jelly on each square.

THE F. A. KLAINE CO.

MANUFACTURERS OF

GOOD WILL
STOVES
AND
RANGES

*FOR
ALL
KINDS
OF
FUEL*

ON SALE AT FIRST-CLASS DEALERS

UNION MADE   HOME PRODUCT

MADE OF THE BEST MATERIAL.
MADE TO LAST.

HICKORY NUT OR WALNUT CAKE.

Two cups of fine white sugar creamed with half a cup of butter, three eggs, two-thirds of a cup of sweet milk, three cups of sifted flour, one heaping teaspoonful of baking powder sifted through the flour; a tablespoonful (level) of powdered mace, a coffeecup of hickory nut or walnut meats chopped a little. Fill the cake-pans with a layer of the cake, then a layer of raisins upon that, then strew over these a handful of nuts, and so on until the pan is two-thirds full. Line the tins with well-buttered paper and bake in a steady, but not quick, oven. This is most excellent.

LAYER JELLY CAKE.

Almost any soft cake recipe can be used for jelly cake. The following is excellent: One cup of sugar, half a cup of butter, three eggs, half a cup of sweet milk, two cups of flour, two heaping teaspoonfuls of baking powder, flavoring.

For white delicate cake the rule for "Silver Cake" is fine, care should be taken, however, that the oven is just right for this cake, as it browns very easily. To be baked in jelly-cake tins in layers, with filling put between when done.

ANGEL CAKE.

Put into one tumbler of flour one teaspoonful of cream of tartar, then sift it five times. Sift also one glass and a half of white powdered sugar. Beat to a stiff froth the whites of eleven eggs; stir the sugar into the eggs by degrees, very lightly and carefully, adding three teaspoonfuls of vanilla extract. After this add the flour, stirring quickly and lightly. Pour it into a clean, bright cake-dish, which should *not* be buttered or lined. Bake at once in a moderate oven about forty minutes, testing it with a broom splint. When done let it remain in the cake-tin, turning it upside down, with the sides resting on the tops of two saucers, so that a current of air will pass under and over it.

This is the best recipe found after trying several. A perfect cake.

MORRIS WHITE

One of Cincinnati's Benefactors.

MARBLE CAKE.

White Part.—Whites of four eggs, one cup of white sugar, half a cup of butter, half a cup of sweet milk, two teaspoonfuls of baking powder, one teaspoonful of vanilla or lemon and two and a half cups of sifted flour.

Dark Part.—Yolks of four eggs, one cup of brown sugar, half a cup of cooking molasses, half a cup of butter, half a cup of sour milk, one teaspoonful of ground cloves, one teaspoonful of cinnamon, one teaspoonful of mace, one nutmeg grated, one teaspoonful of soda, the soda to be dissolved in a little milk and added after part of the flour is stirred in, one and a half cups of sifted flour.

Drop a spoonful of each kind in a well-buttered cake-dish, first the light part, then the dark, alternately. Try to drop it so that the cake shall be well-streaked through, so that it has the appearance of marble.

PLAIN GINGERBREAD.

One cup of *dark* cooking molasses, one cup of sour cream, one egg, one teaspoonful of soda dissolved in a little warm water, a teaspoonful of salt and one heaping teaspoonful of ginger; make about as thick as cup cake. To be eaten warm.

CRANBERRY SAUCE.

One quart of cranberries, two cupfuls of sugar and a pint of water. Wash the cranberries, then put them on the fire with the water, but in a covered saucepan. Let them simmer until each cranberry bursts open; then remove the cover of the saucepan, add the sugar and let them all boil twenty minutes without the cover. The cranberries must never be stirred from the time they are placed on the fire. This is an unfailing recipe for a most delicious preparation of cranberries. Very fine with turkey and game.

FRUIT FILLING.

Four tablespoonfuls of *very finely* chopped citron, four tablespoonfuls of finely chopped seeded raisins, half a cupful of blanched almonds chopped fine, also a quarter of a pound of finely chopped figs. Beat the whites of three eggs to a stiff froth, adding half of a cupful of sugar; then mix thoroughly into this the whole chopped ingredients. Put it between the layers of cake when the cake is *hot*, so that it will cook the egg a little. This will be found delicious.

SPONGE CAKE.

Separate the whites and yolks of six eggs. Beat the yolks to a cream, to which add two teacupfuls of powdered sugar, beating again from five to ten minutes, then add two tablespoonfuls of milk or water, a pinch of salt and flavoring. Now add part of the beaten whites; then two cups of flour in which you have sifted two teaspoonfuls of baking powder; mix gradually into the above ingredients, stirring slowly and lightly, only enough to mix them well; lastly add the remainder of the whites of the eggs. Line the tins with buttered paper and fill two-thirds full.

WHITE MOUNTAIN CAKE.

Cream three cupfuls of sugar and one of butter, making it very light, then add a cupful of milk. Beat the whites of eight eggs very stiff, add half of those to the other ingredients. Mix well into four cups of sifted flour one tablespoonful of baking powder; stir this into the cake, add flavoring, then the remaining beaten whites of egg. Bake in layers like jelly cake. Make an icing for the filling, using the whites of four eggs beaten to a very stiff froth, with two cups of fine white sugar and the juice of half a lemon. Spread each layer of the cake thickly with this icing, place one on another, then ice all over the top and sides.

THE FLETCHER
MOTOR WASHING MACHINE

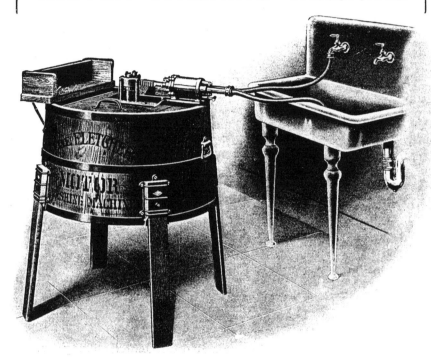

We are agents for this wonderful machine. It is ready for use at all times. Just connect with your faucet and go ahead with the washing. The only machine on the market which *will not tear the clothes.*

Sold on trial to reliable parties.

LOUIS MARX & BROS.
══════LEADING══════
HOME OUTFITTERS

No. 840 Monmouth St., Newport   Nos.516-522 Madison Ave.,Covington

FIG FILLING.

Take a pound of figs, chop fine, and put into a stewpan on the stove; pour over them a teacupful of water and add a half cup of sugar. Cook all together until soft and smooth. When cold spread between layers of cake.

BRIDE'S CAKE.

Cream together one scant cup of butter and three cups of sugar, add one cup of milk, then the beaten whites of twelve eggs; sift three teaspoonful of baking powder into one cup of cornstarch mixed with three cups of sifted flour and beat in gradually with the rest; flavor to taste. Beat all thoroughly, then put in buttered tins lined with letter paper well butter; bake slowly in a *moderate* oven. A beautiful white cake. Ice the top. Double the recipe if more is required.

FRUIT CAKE BY MEASURE. (Very Good.)

Two scant teacupfuls of butter, three cupfuls of dark brown sugar, six eggs, whites and yolks beaten separately, one pound of raisins, seeded, one of currants, washed and dried, and half a pound of citron cut in thin strips; also half a cupful of cooking molasses and half a cupful of sour milk. Stir the butter and sugar to a cream, add to that half a grated nutmeg, one tablespoonful of ground cinnamon, one teaspoonful of cloves, one teaspoonful of mace, add the molasses and sour milk. Stir all well, then put in beaten yolks of eggs, a wine-glass of brandy; stir again all thoroughly, and then add four cupfuls of sifted flour alternately with the beaten whites of eggs. Now dissolve a level teaspoonful of soda and stir in thoroughly. Mix the fruit together and stir into it two heaping tablespoonfuls of flour; then stir it in the cake. Butter two common-sized baking tins carefully, line them with letter paper well buttered, and bake in a moderate oven two hours. After it is baked, let it cool in the pan. Afterward put it into a tight can, or let it remain in the pans and cover tightly. Best recipe of all.

A YOUNG COUPLE Should begin housekeeping by paying attention to QUALITY on all requirements for the **HOME.**

No matter what you buy, if the article has merit, it is the CHEAPEST for HEALTH, HAPPINESS and PROSPERITY.

"DOVE BRAND" Hams, Bacon and Lard. BEST IN THE WORLD

LEMON JELLY FILLING.

Grate the yellow from the rind of two lemons and squeeze out the juice; two cupfuls of sugar, the yolks and whites of two eggs beaten separately. Mix the sugar and yolks, then add the whites and then the lemons. Now pour on a cupful of boiling water, stir into this two tablespoonfuls of sifted flour, rubbed smooth in half a cupful of water; then add a tablespoonful of melted butter; cook until it thickens. When cold, spread between the layers of cake. Oranges can be used in place of lemons.

Another filling of lemon (without cooking) is made of the grated rind and juice of two lemons and the whites of two eggs beaten with one cup of sugar.

ORANGE CAKE FILLING.

Peel two large oranges, remove the seeds, chop them fine, add half a peeled lemon, one cup of sugar and the well-beaten white of an egg. Spread between the layers of "Silver Cake" recipe.

SILVER, OR DELICATE CAKE.

Whites of six eggs, one cupful of sweet milk, two cupfuls of sugar, four cupfuls of sifted flour, two-thirds of a cup of butter, flavoring and two teaspoonfuls of baking powder. Stir the sugar and butter to a cream, then add the milk and flavoring, part of the flour, the beaten whites of eggs, then the rest of the flour. Bake carefully in tins lined with buttered white paper.

When using the whites of eggs for nice cake, the yolks need not be washed; keep them in a cool place and scramble them. Serve on toast or with chipped beef.

GOLD CAKE.

After beating to a cream one cup and a half of butter and two cups of white sugar, stir in the well-whipped yolks of one dozen eggs, four cupfuls of sifted flour, one teaspoonful of baking powder. Favor with lemon. Line the bake-pans with buttered paper and bake in a moderate oven for one hour.

GOOD COOKING

REQUIRES THE INGREDIENTS,
THE RECIPE AND A

JAP KITCHEN CABINET

To try to cook nowadays without one is as
primitive as heating water with hot stones.

NO. 475

A "JAP" is so arranged that everything the recipe calls for, the
ingredients, the utensils, the implements, are all at the finger tips;
no wondering where certain things are, no unnecessary stops to gather
and replace them from a dozen different places.

A "JAP" is almost equal to another pair of hands.

"JAPS" are made by Kitchen Cabinet Specialists. As much
thought is expended on them as on a fine piano. Don't expect "JAP"
completeness in any other make. *Your dealer sells them.*

CINCINNATI SCREEN COMPANY

PATENTEES AND SOLE MANUFACTURERS.

CINCINNATI, O.

DOUGHNUTS OR FRIED CAKES.

Success in making good fried cakes depends as much on the *cooking* as the mixing. In the first place, there should be boiling lard enough to free them from the bottom of the kettle, so that they swim on the top, and the lard should never be so hot as to smoke or so cool as not to be at the boiling point; if it is, they soak grease and are spoiled. If it is at the right heat, the doughnuts will in about ten minutes be of a delicate brown outside and nicely cooked inside. Five or six minutes will cook a cruller. Try the fat by dropping a bit of the dough in first; if it is right, the fat will boil up when it is dropped in. They should be turned over almost constantly, which causes them to rise and brown evenly. When they are sufficiently cooked, raise them from the hot fat and drain them until every drop ceases dripping.

COOKIES.

One cup of butter, two cups of sugar, a *small* teacupful of sweet milk, half a grated nutmeg and five cups of sifted flour, in which there has been sifted with it two teaspoonfuls of baking powder; mix into a soft dough and cut into round cakes; roll the dough as thin as pie crust. Bake in a quick oven a light brown. These can be made of sour milk and a teaspoonful of soda dissolved in it, or sour or sweet cream can be used in place of butter.

Water cookies made the same as above, using water in place of milk. Water cookies keep longer than milk cookies.

CHOCOLATE ECLAIRS.

Make the mixture exactly like the recipe for "Boston Cream Cakes." Spread it on buttered pans in oblong pieces about four inches long and one and a half wide, to be laid about two inches apart; they must be baked in a rather quick oven about twenty-five minutes. As soon as baked ice with chocolate icing, and when this is cold split them on one side and fill with the same cream as "Boston Cream Cakes."

146

EGGS ON TOAST.

Various preparations of eggs can be served on toast, first dipping slices of well-toasted bread quickly in hot salted water, then turning over them scrambled, poached or creamed eggs, all found in the recipes among EGGS.

STEAMED OATMEAL.

To one teacupful oatmeal add a quart of cold water, a teaspoonful of salt; put in a steamer over a kettle of cold water, gradually heat and steam an hour and a half after it begins to cook.

BAVARIAN CREAM WITH FRUIT.

One quart berries, one cup sugar, one-half box gelatine, one half cup cold water, one-half cup boiling water, one pint cream, strawberries or raspberries can be used. Mash the berries with the sugar, and let them stand still the sugar is dissolved ; stain through a fine sieve. Soak the gelatine in the cold water, then dissolve in the boiling water and strain it into the juice. Cool and beat till slightly thickened and add the whipped cream. Mould it in a plain mould, or lined like a charlotte.

CHARLOTTE RUSSE.

Whip one quart of rich cream to a stiff froth and drain well on a nice sieve. To one scant pint of milk add six eggs beaten very light; make very sweet; flavor high with vanilla. Cook over hot water till it is a thick custard. Soak one full ounce of Cox's gelatine in a very little water and warm over hot water. When the custard is very cold beat in lightly the gelatine and the whipped cream. Line the bottom of your mold with buttered paper, the side with sponge cake or lady-fingers fastened together with the white of an egg. Fill with the cream, put in a cold place, or, in summer, on ice. To turn out, dip the mold for a moment in hot water. In draining the whipped cream, all that drips through can be re-whipped.

HOMINY.

Hominy is a preparation of Indian corn, broken or ground, either large or small, and is an excellent breakfast dish in winter or summer. Wash the hominy thoroughly in one or two waters, then cover it with twice its depth of cold water and let it come to a boil slowly. If it be the large hominy, simmer six hours; if the small hominy, simmer two hours. When the water evaporates add hot water; when done it may be eaten with cream, or allowed to become cold and warmed up in a frying pan, using a little butter to prevent burning.

HOMINY.

This form of cereal is very little known and consequently little appreciated in most Northern households. "Big hominy" and "little hominy," as they are called in the South, are staple dishes there and generally take the place of oatmeal, which is apt to be too heating for the climate. The former is called "samp" here. It must be boiled for at least eight hours to be properly cooked, and may then be kept on hand for two or three days and warmed over, made into croquettes or balls, or fried in cakes. The fine hominy takes two or three hours for proper cooking, and should be cooked in a dish set into another of boiling water, and kept steadily boiling until thoroughly soft.

TOAST.

Toast should be made of stale bread, or at least of bread that has been baked a day. Cut smoothly in slices, not more than half an inch thick; if the crust is baked very hard, trim the edges and brown very evenly, but if it happens to burn, that should be scraped off. Toast that is to be served with anything turned over it, should have the slices first dipped quickly in a dish of hot water turned from the boiling teakettle, with a little salt thrown in. Cold biscuits cut in halves, and the under crust sliced off, then browned evenly on both sides, make equally as good toast.

SOFT SOAP.

EXCELLENT FOR CLEANING CARPETS.

Salt of Tartar, 5 cents; powdered borax, 5 cents; ammonia. 5 cents; washing soda, 3 cents; two bars German soap, one bar Ivory, one bucket water. Shave soap fine and dissolve. Add ingredients, let come to a boil, take off stove and cool.

DIRECTIONS FOR MAKING A CHARMING YOUNG LADY.

From a sixteen-year oldpiece offemale loveliness remove all rough edges of effectation, selfishness and conceit. Mix thouroughly with a good supply of common sense, a dash of wit and just a little sauce. Beat well together until very soft and tender; sweeten, but not too much; garnish with beauty and kindly manners, bake in the fire of love and serve as she deserves.

It is having the little things of the household just right that makes the acme of domestic comfort, that lessons necessary friction with things that all of us feel more or less, and helps us to forget our bodies and nerves.

EARLY SLEEP IS MOST RESTFUL RETIRE EARLY

The best sleep is always the early sleep. For this reason to stay up very late often makes one tired and nervous, so that restful sleep is almost impossible. Diet has little influence on sleep, except in so far as it may produce disturbances of digestion and through these of the general balance of health.

The hypnotic effect of certain foods, such as onions, lettuce, milk, etc., it is claimed by reputable physicians, are chiefly imaginary. Even the time of the last meal is of relatively little importance, except that it is well to let this be at least two hours before retiring, that is supposing the last meal to be a moderately heavy one. But even this rule has exceptions, as many healthy laboring men fall asleep over their pipes directly after supper, and children invariably get sleepy after being well-fed in the evening.

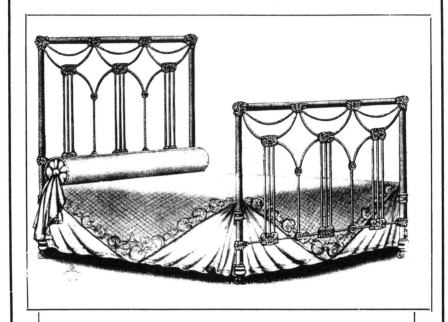

GAME SOUP.

Two Grouse or Partridges, or, if you have neither, use a pair of rabbits; half a pound of lean ham; two medium sized onions; one pound of lean beef; fried bread; butter for frying; pepper, salt, and two stalks of white celery cut into inch lengths; three quarts of water.

Joint your game neatly; cut the ham and onions into small pieces, and fry all in butter to a light brown. Put into a soup-pot with the beef, cut into strips, and a little pepper. Pour on the water heat slowly, and stew gently two hours. Take out the pieces of bird, and cover in a bowl; cook the soup an hour longer; strain; cool; drop in the celery, and simmer ten minutes. Pour upon fried bread in the tureen.

Venison soup made the same, with the addition of a tablespoonful of brown flour wet into a paste with cold water, adding a tablespoonful of catsup, Worcestershire, or other pungent sauce, and a glass of Madeira or brown sherry.

BOSTON BAKED BEANS.

Put one quart small navy beans to soak in cold water over night. In the morning put them in a kettle and boil until the skins will break and roll up when you blow on them. Skim them out and put into a regular earthen bean pot; put one pound of pickled pork, with the rind nicely scored, near the top; have it covered with the beans except the rind; add one tablespoon New Orleans molasses, one teaspoon salt, lump of baking soda as large as a bean, and the same amount of dry mustard. Fill the pot with boiling water and bake slowly for five hours. Keep the pot filled with water until an hour before they are ready to use, then let them get dry, unless you like them very moist. Keep them covered while baking.

SWEET PICKLED PEACHES AND PEARS.

Seven pounds of fruit, three pounds of sugar, one quart of vinegar, one ounce of cloves, one ounce of cinnamon. Scald the vinegar and sugar together and pour on the fruit (while hot) for three mornings; on the fourth scald all together and can.

══ SIMPLICITY ══

in a typewriter secures durability, ease and efficiency of operation, and increases the speed and accuracy of the work: the

UNDERWOOD

STANDARD

TYPEWRITER

IS A

MARVEL

OF

SIMPLICITY

Yet every part is carefully chosen as the best possible means to the perfect finished product.

There is nothing hidden about the Underwood. The type-bars lying when at rest in a compact segment; the patented guide— all parts of which permit the visible writing—which help, not bother, the operator will be shown you, explained also if you like; but really you'll see for yourself why the Underwood *does* endure and why its operation is so easy, quick and accurate.

UNDERWOOD TYPEWRITER COMPANY
INCORPORATED

134 EAST FOURTH ST., CINCINNATI, O.

206A

OX-TAIL SOUP.

Two ox-tails, two slices of ham, one ounce of butter, two carrots, two turnips, three onions, one leek, one head of celery, one bunch of savory herbs, pepper, a tablespoonful of salt, two tablespoonfuls of catsup, one-half glass of port wine, three quarts of water.

Cut up the tails, separating them at the joins; wash them, and put them in the stewpan with the butter. Cut the vegetables in slices and add them with the herbs. Put in one-half pint of water, and stir it over a quick fire until the juices are drawn. Fill up the stewpan with water, and, when boiling, add the salt. Skim well and simmer very gently for four hours, or until the tails are tender. Take them out, skim and strain the soup, thicken with flour, and flavor with the catsup and port wine. Put back the tails, simmer for five minutes and serve.

Another way to make an appetizing ox-tail soup. You should begin to make it the day before you wish to eat the soup. Take two tails, wash clean, and put in a kettle with nearly a gallon of cold water; add a small handful of salt: when the meat is well cooked, take out the bones. Let this stand in a cool room, covered, and next day, about an hour and a half before dinner, skim off the crust or cake of fat which has risen to the top. Add a little onion, carrot, or any vegetables you choose, chopping them fine first; summer savory may also be added.

TOMATO SOUP.

Place in a kettle four pounds of beef. Pour over it one gallon of cold water. Let the meat and water boil slowly for three hours, or until the liquid is reduced to about one-half. Remove the meat and put into the broth a quart of tomatoes, and one chopped onion; salt and pepper to taste. A teaspoonful of flour should be dissolved and stirred in, then allow to boil half an hour longer. Strain and serve hot. Canned tomatoes in place of fresh ones may be used.

VEGETABLE SOUP.

Two pounds of beef, three quarts of water. Cook two hours, then add three potatoes, one pint tomatoes, one-fourth head of cabbage cut fine, two turnips, one cup green corn, two carrots, one-half cup string beans, one handful of macaroni or vermicelli, four tablespoons of rice. A little celery or onion is an improvement. Season to taste, adding a pinch of cayenne pepper. Boil another hour. Send to the table strained, if preferred.

CORN SOUP.

Soupbone, cover with water, boil till meat slips from bone; salt and pepper; keep well skimmed, strain. Add to this stock one pint of grated tomatoes; boil three-quarter hours then add a pint of green corn which has been sliced and scraped from the cob, add three pints of new milk; stir often to prevent scorching. Don't allow it to boil after adding the corn; when near the boiling point remove from fire and add a little rolled cracker.

MOCK TURTLE SOUP.

Scald a well-cleansed calf's head, remove the brain, tie it up in a cloth, and boil an hour, or until the meat will easily slip from the bone; take out, save the broth; cut in small square pieces, and throw them into cold water; when cool, put it in a stewpan, and cover with some of the broth; let it boil until quite tender, and set aside.

In another stewpan melt some butter, and in it put a quarter of a pound of lean ham, cut small, with fine herbs to taste; also parsley and one onion; add about a pint of the broth; let it simmer for two hours, and then dredge in a small quantity of flour; now add the remainder of the broth, and a quarter bottle of Madeira or sherry; let all stew quietly for ten minutes and rub it through a medium sieve; add the calf's head, season with a very little cayenne pepper, a little salt, the juice of one lemon, and, if desired, a quarter teaspoonful pounded mace and a dessert-spoon sugar.

Having previously prepared force meat balls, add them to the soup, and five minutes after serve hot.

THE M. J. CUNNING CO.

14 & 16 E. FOURTH ST.
4TH FLOOR.
OPPOSITE SINTON HOTEL

THE ART NEEDLEWORK STORE OF CINCINNATI.

DESIGNING & STAMPING

LARGEST MANUFACTURERS OF PERFORATED STAMPING PATTERNS IN THE WORLD.

VISIT OUR STORE, SEE OUR LINE COMPRISING LADIES NECKWEAR, EXQUISTE LACES, FINE LINENS, LAWNES, BRAIDS, STAMPED SHIRT WAISTS, CORSET COVERS, CENTER PILLOWS, ETC. ETC.
SILK AND COTTON THREADS.

DAINTY HAND EMBROIDERY A SPECIALTY.

SEND FOR OUR CATALOGUE.
IT IS FREE.

GREEN TURTLE SOUP.

One turtle, two onions, a bunch of sweet herbs, juice of one lemon, five quarts of water, a glass of Madeira.

After moving the entrails, cut up the coarser parts of the turtle meat and bones. Add four quarts of water, and stew four hours with the herbs, onions, pepper and salt. Stew very slowly, do not let it cease boiling during this time. At the end of four hours strain the soup, and add the finer parts of the turtle and the green fat, which has been simmered one hour in two quarts of water. Thicken with brown flour; return to the soup pot, and simmer gently for an hour longer. If there are eggs in the turtle, boil them in a separate vessel for four hours, and throw into the soup before taking up. If not, put in force meat balls; then the juice of the lemon, and the wine; beat up at once and pour out.

Some cooks add the finer meat before straining, boiling all together five hours; then strain, thicken and put in the green fat, cut into lumps an inch long. This makes a handsomer soup than if the meat is left in.

Green turtle can now be purchased preserved in air-tight cans.

Force meat balls for the above.—Six teaspoonfuls of turtle meat chopped very fine. Rub to a paste, with the yolk of two hard-boiled eggs, a teaspoonful of butter, and, if convenient, a little oyster liquor, Season with cayenne, mace, half a teaspoonful of white sugar and a pinch of salt. Bind all with a well-beaten egg; shape into small balls; dip in egg, then powdered cracker; fry in butter, and drop into the soup when it is served.

VEGETABLE SOUP.

Scrape and slice three turnips and three carrots and peel there onions, and fry all with a little butter until a light yellow; add a bunch of celery and three or four leeks cut in pieces; stir and fry all the ingredients for six minutes; when fried, add one clove of garlic, two stalks of parsley, two cloves, salt, pepper and a little grated nutmeg; cover with three quarts of water and simmer for three hours, taking off the scum carefully. Strain and use. Croutons vermicelli, Italian pastes, or rice may be added.

FOURTH STREET CINCINNATI EAST FROM RACE STREET.

160

BEEF SOUP.

Select a small shin of beef of moderate size, crack the bone in small pieces, wash and place it in a kettle to boil, with five or six quarts of *cold* water. Let it boil about two hours, or until it begins to get tender, then season it with a tablespoonful of salt, and a teaspoonful of pepper; boil it one hour longer, then add to it one carrot, two turnips, two tablespoonfuls of rice or pearl barley, one head of celery, and a teaspoonful of summer savory powdered fine; the vegetables to be minced up in small pieces like dice. After these ingredients have boiled a quarter of an hour, put in two potatoes cut up in small pieces; let it boil half an hour longer; take the meat from the soup, and if intended to be served with it, take out the bones and lay it closely and neatly on a dish, and garnish with sprigs of parsley.

Serve made mustard and catsup with it. It is very nice pressed and eaten cold with mustard and vinegar, or catsup. Four hours are required for making this soup. Should any remain over the first day, it may be heated, **with** the addition of a little boiling water, and served again. Some fancy a glass of brown sherry added just before being served. Serve very hot.

NOODLES.

Beat up one egg light, add a pinch of salt, and flour enough to make a *very stiff* dough; roll out very thin, like thin pie crust, dredge with flour to keep from sticking. Let it remain on the bread board to dry for an hour or more; then roll it up in a tight scroll, like a sheet of music. Begin at the end and slice it into slips as thin as straws. After all are cut, mix then all together, and to prevent them sticking, keep them floured a little until you are ready to drop them in to boil, which should be done shortly before dinner, for if boiled *too long* they will go to pieces.

"We clothe them all"

THE CHILDREN'S SHOP

OUTFITS FOR CHILDREN AND INFANTS
MISSES' UP-TO-DATE SUITS AND DRESSES

SUITE 205 AND 207 ANDREWS BUILDING

FIFTH & RACE STREETS   CINCINNATI, O.

CHOW CHOW.

Cabbage and Tomatoes. Take one-half and one-third (?) green tomatoes and cabbage, the former cut each way, fine, and the cabbage as fine as possible, season to taste with salt, Dove Brand Pepper and Dove Brand Spice, to one gallon of the chow chow add one-half gallon vinegar; cook till soft, and seal up, it will keep a long time.

CHOW CHOW.

Two heads of cauliflower, two heads of cabbage, a gallon of string beans, three quarts of green tomatoes, four quarts tiny cucumbers, and the same amount of little onions. Chop the cabbage, but not finely, break the cauliflower in its component parts, mix all and stir thoroughly the whole and a quart of salt, in the morning pour cold water over, and drain; repeat the process, and drain again; even a third bath will not be to much. Then stir into the mixture already prepared two ounces Dove Brand White Mustard Seed, two and one-half ounces Dove Brand Celery Seed and two heaping table-spoonfuls Dove Brand Ground Mustard. Cover with vinegar, and boil thirty minutes. Just before taking from the stove pour in one-half pound of sugar. This will keep without sealing, but is better sealed.

CHUTNEY SAUCE.

Twelve green sour apples, two green peppers, six green tomatoes, four small onions, one cupful raisins, one quart vinegar, two table-spoonfuls Dove Brand Mustard Seed, two of salt, one of powdered sugar, two cupfuls brown sugar. Remove the seeds from the raisins and peppers, then add the tomatoes and onions, and chop all very fine. Put the vinegar, sugar and spices to boil, add the chopped mixture, and simmer one hour. Then add the apples, pared and cored, and cook slowly until soft. Keep it in a small bottle well sealed.

SWEET CUCUMBER PICKLE.

Pare and cut the cucumbers and scrape out the seeds. Put the pieces in a stone jar and cover with salt and water (not to strong) let stand for two days, changing the water every day; take them out and let drain, then let them stand four or five hours in fresh water, then boil them in vinegar until tender, take them out carefully and put in a stone jar. Make a syrup of one quart of vinegar, four pounds sugar, one ounce Dove Cassia buds, and a tablespoon of Dove Brand Cinnamon; boil until the syrup is clear and pour over the cucumbers. The amount of syrup mentioned above is enough for three to four quarts of cucumbers after they are boiled.

SOUR CUCUMBER PICKLE.

Delicious. Pick small cucumbers. Make a weak brine and pour over scalding hot three successive mornings, making new brine each morning. Then pour boiling water over three mornings. Pack cucumbers in a jar with a few Dove Brand Cloves and Dove Brand Spices, (spiced vinegar) and then pour over scalding hot vinegar, and season.

PICKLETTE.

If sweet? Cabbage. Peel and chop six large white onions, one large head of white cabbage. Arrange these in a stone crock in alternate layers, sprinkle each layer with a little salt, and allow to stand twenty-four hours. The next morning place one pint of good cider vinegar in a preserving kettle and add one-half pound brown sugar, a heaping teaspoonful each of Dove Brand Powdered Alum, Dove Brand Tumeric, Dove Brand Ground Cinnamon, Dove Brand Allspice, Dove Brand Mace, Dove Brand Black Pepper, Dove Brand Mustard and Dove Brand Celery Seed; allow all to come to a boil. Pour this over the chopped vegetables, and let stand for twenty-four hours, then drain off the vinegar, heat again to boiling and again pour over the vegetables. Repeat this process for three mornings in succession. On the fourth morning place all together in the preserving kettle, boil five minutes and then pack in small jars and seal when cold.

166

HOTCH POTCH PICKLE.

One large head cabbage, two dozen cucumbers, one dozen green tomatoes, three green peppers, chop all fine. Take one-half dozen white onions, slice, pour boiling water over them and let stand fifteen minutes, then mix with the other ingredients, add one-half cupful salt, let stand one hour. Then drain off all the juice, and cover with weak vinegar twenty-four hours. The next morning drain again, and to every gallon of pickles put one-half pound brown sugar, one ounce each Dove Brand Pepper, Dove Brand Cloves, and Dove Brand White Mustard Seed; if you like Celery, add one-half ounce Dove Brand Celery Seed. Put all in a kettle, cover with good vinegar, boil one-half hour. Put in jars.

AN EXCELLENT CELERY PICKLE.

Cabbage. Select a very solid white head of cabbage. Chop the center, then chop an equal amount of white celery. Put both in a porcelain-lined kettle, add two tablespoonfuls salt, a quarter-pound Dove Brand White Mustard Seed, a quarter ounce Dove Brand Ginger Root sliced, and two quarts good cider vinegar. For this quantity there should be two quarts of cabbage and two quarts of celery. Stand over a moderate fire until the whole mess is thoroughly heated. When cold put into stone or glass jars for keeping.

PICCALILLI.

Two quarts tomatoes, two quarts cucumbers, one-half pint peppers, one pint onions, chop; then put in stone jars with a cupful salt in them, and let stand twenty-four hours, then while draining take two quarts of vinegar and two cupfuls brown sugar; scald, adding a bag of all kinds of Dove Brand Whole Spices, drain, and put back into chopped mixture, and soak two hours.

FINE PICKLED CABBAGE.

Shred red and white cabbage. Spread it in layers in a stone jar with salt over each layer. Put two spoonfuls whole Dove Brand Black Pepper, and the same quantity each of Dove Brand Allspice, Dove Brand Cloves and Dove Brand Cinnamon in a bag, and scald in two quarts vinegar. Put this vinegar over the cabbage and cover it tight. It will be ready for use in two days.

168

Dinner Giving

The Laying of the Table and the Treatment of the Guests.

In giving "dinners" the apparently trifling details are of great importance when taken as a whole.

There are certain established laws by which "dinner giving" is regulated in polite society; and it may not be amiss to give a few observances in relation to them. One of the first is that an invited guest should arrive at the house of his host at least a quarter of an hour before the time appointed for dinner. In laying the table for dinner *all* the linen should be a spotless white throughout, and underneath the linen tablecloth should be spread one of thick cotton flannel or baize which gives the linen a heavier and finer appearance, also deadening the sound of moving dishes. Large and neatly folded napkins (ironed without starch). An ornamental centre-piece, or a vase filled with a few rare flowers, is put on the centre of the table. A few choice flowers make a charming variety in the appearance of even the mostly simply laid table, for the eyes in fact should be gratified as much as the palate.

Beside each plate should be laid as many knives, forks and spoons as will be required for the several courses, unless the hostess prefers to have them brought on with each change. A glass of water, and when wine is served glasses for it, and individual salt-cellars may be placed at every plate. Water-bottles are now much in vogue with corresponding tumblers to cover them; these, accompanied with dishes of broken ice, may be arranged in suitable places. When butter is served a special knife is used.

The dessert plates should be set ready, each with a doily and a finger-glass partly filled with water, in which is dropped a slice of lemon; these with extra knives, forks and spoons, should be on the side-board ready to be placed beside the guest between the courses when required.

ANNOUNCEMENTS
CARDS   INVITATIONS
PROGRAMMES

OUR FACILITIES AND EQUIPMENT ARE INCOMPARABLE

REMEMBER!

OPPORTUNITIES COME TO ALL MEN WHO HUSTLE

THE F. C. H. MANNS CO.
PRINTERS   DESIGNERS   ENGRAVERS

9TH FLOOR   COMMERCIAL TRIBUNE BUILDING

If preferred, the "dinner" may all be served from the side-table, thus relieving the host from the task of carving. A plate is set before each guest, and the dish carved is presented by the waiter on the left-hand side of each guest. At the end of each course the plates give way for those of the next. If not served from the side-table, the dishes are brought in ready carved, and placed before the host and hostess, then served and placed upon the waiter's salver, to be laid by that attendant before the guest.

Soup and fish being the first course, plates of soup are usually placed on the table before the dinner is announced; or if the hostess wishes the soup served at the table, the soup-tureen, containing *hot* soup, and the *warm* soup-plates are placed before the seat of the hostess. Soup and fish being disposed of, then come the joints or roasts, *entrees* (made dishes), po^rltry, etc., also relishes.

After dishes have been passed that are required no more, they may be set upon the side-board, ready to be taken away.

Jellies and sauces, when not to be eaten as a dessert, should be helped on the dinner-plate.

If a dish be on the table, some parts of which are preferred to others, according to the taste of the individuals, all should have the opportunity of choice. The host will simply ask each one if he has any preference for a particular part; if he replies in the negative, you are not to repeat the question, nor insist that he must have a preference.

Do not attempt to eulogize your dishes, or apologize that you cannot recommend them—this is extreme bad taste; as also is the vaunting of the excellence of your wines, etc.

Do not insist upon your guests partaking of particular dishes. Do not ask persons more than once, and never force a supply upon their plates. It is ill-bred, though common, to press any one to eat; it is a great annoyance to many.

In winter, plates should be warmed, but not made hot. Two kinds of animal food, or two kinds of dessert, should not be eaten off of one plate, and there should never be more than two kinds of vegetables with one course. Asparagus, green corn, cauliflower and raw tomatoes comprise one course in place of a salad. All meats should be cut across the grain in very thin slices. Fish, at dinner, should be baked or boiled, never fried or broiled. Baked ham may be used in every course after fish, sliced thin and handed after the regular course is disposed of.

The hostess should retain her plate, knife and fork, until her guests have finished.

The crumb-brush is not used until the preparation for bringing in the dessert; then all the glasses are removed, except the flowers, the water-tumblers, and the glass of wine which the guest wishes to retain with his dessert. The dessert plate containing the finger-bowl, also a dessert knife and fork, should then be set before each guest, who at once removes the finger-bowl and its doily, and the knife and fork to the table, leaving the plate ready to be used for any dessert chosen.

Finely sifted powdered sugar should always be placed upon the table to be used with puddings, pies, fruits, etc., and if cream is required, let it stand by the dish it is to be served with.

To lay a dessert for a small entertainment and a few guests outside of the family, it may consist simply of two dishes of fresh fruit in season, two of dried fruits and two each of cakes and nuts.

Coffee and tea are served *lastly*, passed around to each guest, then the sugar and cream passed that each person may be allowed to season his black coffee or *cafe noir* to suit himself.

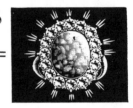

174

TOMATO CATSUP.

Put into two quarts of tomato pulp (or two cans of canned tomatoes) one onion, cut fine, two tablespoonfuls of salt and three tablespoonfuls of brown sugar. Boil until quite thick; then take from the fire and strain it through a sieve, working it until it is all through but the seeds. Put it back on the stove, and add two tablespoonfuls of mustard, one of allspice, one of black pepper and one of cinnamon, one teaspoonful of ground cloves, half a teaspoonful of cayenne pepper, one grated nutmeg, one pint of good vinegar boil it until it will just run from the mouth of a bottle. It should be watched, stirred often, that it does not burn. If sealed tight while *hot*, in large-mouthed bottles, it will keep good for years.

CHICKEN A LA MACARONI OR SPAGHETTI.

Brown two spring chickens in butter, season well, and when they have become a nice brown drain off the butter and replace with a wine glass of white wine, then add a small cupful of consomme and allow to cook until the chickens are done. Add a 5c. package of Wuerdeman's Macaroni or Spaghetti which has been boiled in two quarts of water, with a handful of mushrooms. Arrange the chickens on a dish with the garnishings around and pour the gravy over the whole.

BOILED MACARONI OR SPAGHETTI.

Three-fourths cup of Macaroni broken in 1-inch pieces, one-half cup cream, one tablespoonful of salt, two quarts boiling water. Cook Macaroni or Spaghetti in boiling salted water twenty minutes, or until tender, drain in strainer, pour over it cold water to prevent pieces from adhering, add cream, reheat and season.

MACARONI OR SPEGHETTI with WHITE SAUCE.

Cook as for boiled Macaroni or Spaghetti, Wuerdeman's 5 c package, but in place of cream add *White Sauce* made as follows: Melt two tablespoons of butter, add two tablespoons flour, with one-half teaspoonful salt, and pour on slowly one and one-half cups scalded milk.

MACARONI OR SPAGHETTI PUDDING.

Empty a 5c. package of Wuerdeman's Macaroni or Spaghetti in rapidly boiling salt water until tender, drain through a colander. Put them in a baking dish. To three well beaten eggs add a quart of milk, two tablespoonfuls of sugar, one tablespoonful of cinnamon or one tablespoonful of vanilla. Pour over the macaroni and bake in a well-heated oven one-half hour. This is an inexpensive and delicious dish, and will serve at least ten persons.

MACARONI OR SPAGHETTI
with TOMATO SAUCE.

Empty a 5c. package of Wuerdeman's Macaroni or Spaghetti in rapidly boiling hot water, drain through a colander, and pour cold water over it to keep them from adhering. Open a can of tomatoes, put into it the tops of celery cut in fine pieces, boil this well and press through a colander. Add to this one tablespoonful of butter, one teaspoonful of sugar, pepper to taste, add macaroni or spaghetti to sauce and let simmer from ten to fifteen minutes.

MACARONI OR SPAGHETTI
with SLICED TOMATOES.

Boil the contents of a 5c. package of Wuerdeman's Macaroni or Spaghetti in two quarts of salted boiling water twenty minutes; when about done add a teaspoonful of salt, drain, pour cold water over and drain again, to prevent them from adhering. Butter a baking dish, put a layer of macaroni or spaghetti at the bottom, sprinkle salt and pepper and pieces of butter, then a layer of sliced tomatoes and bread crumbs; repeat these layers alternately, making the last layer tomatoes; bread crumbs bits of butter, salt and pepper to taste.

BAKED MACARONI OR SPAGHETTI.

Put Macaroni or Spaghetti, Wuerdeman's 5 c. package, with white sauce in a buttered pan, or baking dish, cover with buttered crumbs and bake till crumbs are brown.

ASK FOR

WUERDEMAN'S

MACARONI,
SPAGHETTI
AND
HOME-MADE
EGG NOODLES

"Taste Delicious, Is Nutritious."

ABSOLUTELY PURE AND FREE FROM ADULTERATION

When you want good Macaroni, ask your grocer for **Wuerdeman's Famous White Dove Brand.** Positively the Best that is Made.

Don't forget our **Sunshine Brand, Leon Geffroid French Style Macaroni and Spaghetti,** manufactured of the best Semolina flour

PATRONIZE THE
QUEEN CITY FACTORY

THE WUERDEMAN CO.
427, 429, 431 E. PEARL ST., CINCINNATI. O.

BAKED MACARONI OR SPAGHETTI
with CHEESE.

Boil a 5c. package of Wuerdeman's Macaroni or Spaghetti in two quarts of boiling salt water for twenty minutes, drain through a colander and pour cold water over them to blanch them. Put in a greased baking dish a layer of macaroni or spaghetti, then a layer of bread crumbs, a layer of cheese, grated, sprinkle with salt and pepper, add pieces of butter over this; continue these layers alternately, making the last layer of cheese; then pour a cupful of milk over it and bake fully one-half hour.

MACARONI OR SPAGHETTI with TOMATO
SAUCE and MUSHROOMS.

Boil the contents of Wuerdeman's Macaroni or Spaghetti in two quarts of boiling water about one-half hour, drain in colander and let cold water run over them. Prepare a sauce, by boiling a can of tomatoes in a sauce pan with a small onion and then press through a colander. Add a cupful of mushrooms to this sauce and season to taste. Pour this over the macaroni and heat again. Then serve.

MACARONI OR SPAGHETTI with CHEESE.

Put a layer of boiled Macaroni or Spaghetti, Wuerdeman's 5 c. package, in a buttered baking dish, sprinkle with grated cheese, season with salt, cayenne pepper and mustard, cover with warm milk until milk can be seen through Macaroni or Spaghetti. Sprinkle top with grated cheese. Bake in slow oven until cheese is brown.

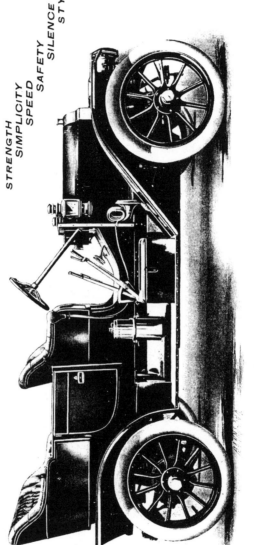

OHIO MODEL 40

THE MODERATE-PRICED CAR HAVING ALL THE
DESIRABLE FEATURES DEMANDED BY
CRITICAL AUTOMOBILE OWNERS—

STRENGTH
SIMPLICITY
SPEED
SAFETY
SILENCE
STYLE

BUILT BY **THE JEWEL CARRIAGE COMPANY**

MANUFACTURERS OF _QUALITY_ VEHICLES   CINCINNATI, U. S. A.

ELMWOOD STATION

MUSHROOM SAUCE.

Wash a pint of small button mushrooms, remove the stems and outside skins, stew them slowly in veal gravy or milk or cream, adding an onion, and seasoning with pepper, salt and a little butter rolled in flour. Their flavor will be heightened by salting a few the night before, to extract the juice. In dressing mushrooms, only those of a dull pearl color on the outside and the under part tinged with pale pink should be selected. If there is a poisonous one among them, the onion in the sauce will turn black. In such a case throw the whole away. Used for poultry, beef or fish.

APPLE SAUCE.

When you wish to serve apple sauce with meat prepare it in this way: Cook the apples until they are very tender, then stir them thoroughly so there will be no lumps at all; add the sugar and a little gelatine dissolved in warm water, a tablespoonful in a pint of sauce; pour the sauce into bowls, and when cold it will be stiff like jelly, and can be turned out on a plate. Cranberry sauce can be treated in the same way. Many prefer this to a plain stewing.

Apples cooked in the following way look very pretty on a tea-table, and are appreciated by the palate. Select firm, round green-ings; pare neatly and cut in halves; place in a shallow stewpan with sufficient boiling water to cover them, and a cupful of sugar to every six apples. Each half should cook on the bottom of the pan, and be removed from the others so as not to injure its shape. Stew slowly until the pieces are very tender; remove to a dish carefully; boil the syrup half an hour longer; pour it over the apples and eat cold. A few pieces of lemon boiled in the syrup adds to the flavor. These sauces are a fine accomplishment to roast pork or roast goose.

RASPBERRY VINEGAR.

Three quarts berries, one-half gallon wine vinegar; let stand four days, then strain twice. To each pint of vinegar add one pint of loaf sugar. When dissolved it is ready for use.

182

PICKLED ONIONS.

Peel small onions until they are white. Scald them in salt and water until tender, then take them up, put them into wide-mouthed bottles, and pour over them hot spiced vinegar; when cold, cork them close. Keep in a dry, dark place. A tablespoonful of sweet oil may be put in the bottles before the cork. The best sort of onions for pickling are the small white buttons.

PICKLED MANGOES.

Let the mangoes or young musk-melons, lie in salt water, strong enough to bear an egg, for two weeks; then soak them in pure water for two days, changing the water two or three times; then remove the seeds and put the mangoes in a kettle, first a layer of grape leaves, then mangoes, and so on until all are in, covering the top with leaves; add a lump of alum the size of a hickory nut; pour vinegar over them and boil them ten or fifteen minutes; remove the leaves and let the pickles stand in this vinegar for a week; then stuff them with the following mixture: One pound of ginger soaked in brine for a day or two, and cut in slices, one ounce of black pepper, one of mace, one of allspice, one of tumeric, half a pound of garlic, soaked for a day or two in brine and then dried; one pint grated horse-radish, one of black mustard seed and one of white mustard seed; bruise all the spices and mix with a teacup of pure olive oil; to each mango add one teaspoonful of brown sugar; cut one solid head of cabbage fine; add one pint of small onions, a few small cucumbers and green tomatoes; lay them in brine a day and a night, then drain them well and add the imperfect mangoes chopped fine and the spices; mix thoroughly, stuff the mangoes and tie them; put them in a stone jar and pour over them the best cider vinegar; set them in a bright, dry place until they are canned. In a month add three pounds of brown sugar; if this is not sufficient, add more until agreeable to taste. This is for four dozen mangoes.

TOMATO SAUCE.

Take a quart can of tomatoes, put it over the fire in a stewpan, put in one slice of onion and two cloves, a little pepper and salt; boil about twenty minutes; then remove it from the fire and strain it through a sieve.   Now melt in another pan one ounce of butter, and as it melts, sprinkle in a tablespoonful of flour; stir it until it browns and froths a little.   Mix the tomato pulp with it, and it is ready for the table.

Excellent for mutton chops, roast beef, etc.

CHILI SAUCE.

Boil together two dozen ripe tomatoes, three small green peppers, or a half teaspoonful of cayenne pepper, one onion cut fine, half a cup of sugar.   Boil until thick; then add two cups of vinegar; then strain the whole, set back on the fire and add a tablespoonful of salt, and a teaspoonful each of ginger, allspice, cloves and cinnamon; boil all five minutes, remove and seal in glass bottles.   This is very nice.

MINT SAUCE.

Take fresh young spearmint leaves stripped from the stems; wash and drain them, or dry on a cloth.   Chop very fine, put in a gravy boat, and to three tablespoonfuls of mint put two of white sugar; mix and let it stand a few minutes, then pour over it six tablespoonfuls of good cider or white-wine vinegar.   The sauce is to be made some time before it is to be used, so that the flavor of the mint may be well extracted.   Fine with roast lamb.

WINE SAUCE FOR GAME.

Half a glass of currant jelly, half a glass of port wine, half a glass of water, a tablespoonful of cold butter, a teaspoonful of salt, the juice of half a lemon, a pinch of cayenne pepper and three cloves. Simmer all together a few minutes, adding the wine after it is strained.   A few spoonfuls of the gravy from the game may be added to it.   This sauce is especially nice with venison.

AVONDALE PUBLIC SCHOOL, CINCINNATI.

ROAST QUARTER OF LAMB.

Procure a nice hind-quarter, remove some of the fat that is around the kidney, skewer the lower joint up to the fillet, place it in a moderate oven, let it heat through slowly, then dredge it with salt and flour; quicken the fire, put half a pint of water into the dripping-pan, with a teaspoonful of salt. With this liquor baste the meat occasionally; serve with lettuce, green peas and mint sauce.

A quarter of lamb weighing seven or eight pounds will require two hours to roast.

A breast of lamb roasted is very sweet, and is considered by many as preferable to hind-quarter. It requires nearly as long a time to roast as the quarter, and should be served in the same manner.

Make the gravy from the drippings, thickened with flour.

The mint sauce is made as follows: Take fresh, young spearmint leaves stripped from stems; wash and drain them or dry on a cloth, chop very fine, put in a gravy tureen, and to three tablespoonfuls of mintadd two of fine powdered cut-loaf sugar; mix, and let it stand a few minutes, then pour over it six tablespoonfuls good cider or white-wine vinegar. The sauce should be made some time before dinner, so that the flavor of the mint may be well extracted.

LAMB STEW.

Cut up the lamb into small pieces (after removing all the fat) say about two inches square. Wash it well and put it over the fire, with just enough cold water to cover it well, and let it heat gradually. It should stew gently until it is partly done, then add a few thin slices of salt pork, one or two onions sliced up fine, some pepper and salt if needed, and two or three raw potatoes cut up into inch pieces. Cover it closely and stew until the meat is tender. Drop in a few made dumplings, made like short biscuit, cut out *very* small. Cook fifteen minutes longer. Thicken the gravy with a little flour moistened with milk. Serve.

GILLETTE SAFETY RAZORS

BAROMETERS	RACE GLASSES
THERMOMETERS	TELESCOPES
OPERA GLASSES	TORIC LENSES
FIELD GLASSES	MAGNIFYING GLASSES

AUTOMOBILE GOGGLES

CONKLINS SELF FILLING FOUNTAIN PENS

Kryptoks are bifocal glasses without the objectionable appearance commonly associated with bifocals and are made to fit the near and far vision requirements of any individual.

They are by far the most elegant in appearance the most serviceable and the only perfect bifocal lenses. Made by

THE STANDARD OPTICAL CO.

C. A. CULBERTSON
PRES AND TREAS.

13 ARCADE

ROAST LOIN OF PORK.

Score the skin in strips about a quarter of an inch apart; place it in a dripping-pan with a *very little* water under it; cook it moderately at first; as a high heat hardens the rind before the meat is heated through. If it is very lean, it should be rubbed with fresh lard or butter when put into the pan. A stuffing might be made of bread crumbs, chopped sage and onions, pepper and salt, and baked separately on a pie dish; this method is better than putting it in the meat, as many persons have a great aversion to its flavor. A loin weighing about six pounds will roast in about two hours; allow more time if it should be very fat. Make a gravy with flour stirred n *t* o the pork drippings. Serve with apple sauce and pickles.

ROAST SPARERIB.

Trim off the rough ends neatly, crack the ribs across the middle, rub with salt and sprinkle with pepper, fold over, stuff with turkey dressing, sew up tightly, place in a dripping-pan with a pint of water, baste frequently, turning over once so as to bake both sides equally until a rich brown.

PORK TENDERLOINS.

The tenderloins are unlike any other part of the pork in flavor. They may be either fried or broiled; the latter being drier, require to be well-buttered before serving, which should be done on a hot platter before the butter becomes oily. Fry them in a little lard, turning them to have them cooked through; when done, remove, and keep hot while making a gravy by dredging a little flour into the hot fat; if not enough add a little butter or lard, stir until browned, and add a little milk or cream, stir briskly, and pour over the dish. A little Worcestershire sauce may be added to the gravy if desired.

HADDON HALL, AVONDALE, CINCINNATI

PORK CHOPS AND FRIED APPLES.

Season the chops with salt and pepper and a little powdered sage; dip them into bread crumbs. Fry about twenty minutes or until they are done. Put them on a hot dish; pour off part of the gravy into another pan to make a gravy to serve with them, if you choose. Then fry apples which you have sliced about two-thirds of an inch thick, cutting them around the apple so that the core is in the centre of each piece; then cut out the core. When they are browned on one side and partly cooked, turn them carefully with a pancake turner, and finish cooking; dish around the chops or on a separate dish.

BOSTON PORK AND BEANS.

Pick over carefully a quart of small white beans; let them soak over night in cold water; in the morning wash and drain in another water. Put on to boil in plenty of cold water with a piece of soda the size of a bean; let them come to a boil then drain again, cover with water once more, and boil them fifteen minutes, or until the skin of the beans will crack open when taken out and blown upon. Drain the beans again, put them into an earthen pot, adding a tablespoonful of salt; cover with hot water, place in the center of a pound of salt pork, first scalding it with hot water, and scoring the rind across the top, a quarter of an inch apart to indicate where the slices are to be cut. Place the pot in the oven, and bake six hours or longer. Keep the oven a moderate heat; add hot water from the tea-kettle as needed, on account of evaporation, to keep the beans moist. When the meat becomes crisp and looks cooked, remove it, as too long baking the pork destroys its solidity.

IRISH STEW.

Time about two hours. Two and a half pounds of chops, eight potatoes, four turnips, four small onions, nearly a quart of water. Take some chops from loin of mutton, place them in a stewpan in alternate layers of sliced potatoes and chops; add turnips and onions cut into pieces, pour in nearly a quart of cold water; cover stewpan closely, let it stew gently till vegetables are ready to mash and the greater part of the gravy is absorbed; then place in a dish; serve it up hot.

ROAST PIG.

Prepare your dressing as for dressing for fowls, adding half an onion, chopped fine; set it inside. Take a young pig about six weeks old, wash it thoroughly inside and outside; and in another water put a teaspoonful of baking soda, and rinse out the inside again; wipe it dry with a fresh towel, salt the inside and stuff it with the prepared dressing; making it full and plump, giving it its original size and shape. Sew it up, place it in a kneeling posture in the dripping-pan, tying the legs in proper position. Pour a little hot salted water into the dripping-pan, baste with butter and water a few times as the pig warms, afterwards with gravy from the dripping-pan. When it begins to smoke all over rub it often with a rag dipped in melted butter. This will keep the skin from cracking and it still will be crisp. It will take from two to three hours to roast. Make the gravy by skimming off most of the grease, stir into that remaining in the pan a good tablespoon of flour, turn in water to make it the right consistency, season with pepper and let all boil up once. Strain, and if you like wine in it, add half a glass; turn it into a gravy boat. Place the pig upon a large, hot platter, surronded with parsley or celery tops; place a green wreath around the neck, and a sprig of celery in its mouth. In carving, cut off its head first; split down the back, take off its hams and shoulders, and seperate the ribs.

TO BAKE A HAM.

Take a medium-sized ham and place it to soak for ten or twelve hours. Then cut away the rusty part from underneath, wipe it dry, and cover it rather thickly over with a paste made of flour and water. Put it into an earthen dish, and set it in a moderately heated oven. When done, take off the crust carefully, and peel off the skin, put a frill of cut paper around the knuckle, and raspings of bread over the fat of the ham, or serve it glazed and garnished with cut vegetables. It will take about four or five hours to bake it.

Cooked in this way the flavor is much finer than when boiled.

PIG'S FEET PICKLED.

Take twelve pig's feet, scrape and wash them clean, put them into a saucepan with enough hot (not boiling) water to cover them. When partly done, salt them. It requires four to five hours to boil them soft. Pack them in a stone crock, and pour over them spiced vinegar made hot. They will be ready to use in a day or two. If you wish them for breakfast, split them, make a batter of two eggs, a cup of milk, salt, a teaspoonful of butter, with flour enough to make a thick batter; dip each piece in this and fry in hot lard. Or, dip them in beaten egg and flour and fry. Souse is good eaten cold or warm.

TO FRY OUT LARD.

Skin the leaf lard carefully, cut it into small pieces, and put it into a kettle or saucepan, pour in a cupful of water to prevent burning; set it over the fire where it will melt slowly. Stir it frequently and let it simmer until nothing remains but brown scraps. Remove the scraps with a perforated skimmer, throw in a little salt to settle the fat, and, when clear strain through a coarse cloth into jars. Remember to watch it constantly, stirring it from the bottom until the salt is thrown in to settle it, then set it back on the range until clear. If it scorches it gives it a very bad flavor.

FAIRMOUNT PUBLIC SCHOOL, CINCINNATI

ROAST BEEF.

One very essential point in roasting beef is to have the oven well heated when the beef is first put in; this causes the pores to close up quickly, and prevents the escape of the juices.

Take a rib piece or loin roast of seven or eight pounds. Wipe it thoroughly all over with a clean wet towel. Lay it in a dripping-pan, and baste it well with butter or suet fat. Set it in the oven. Baste it frequently with its own drippings, which will make it brown and tender. When partly done season with salt and pepper, as it hardens any meat to salt it when raw, and draws out its juices, then dredge with sifted flour to give it a frothy appearance. It will take a roast of this size about two hours' time to be properly done, leaving the inside a little rare or red—half an hour less would make the inside quite rare. Remove the beef to a heated dish, set where it will keep hot; then skim the drippings from all fat, add a table-spoonful of sifted flour, a little pepper and a teacupful of boiling water. Boil up once and serve hot in a gravy boat.

Some prefer the clear gravy without the thickening. Serve with mustard or grated horse-radish and vinegar.

BEEFSTEAK.

The first consideration in broiling is to have a clear, glowing bed of coals. The steak should be about three-quarters of an inch in thickness, and should be pounded only in extreme cases, i. e., when it is cut *too* thick and is "stringy." Lay it on a buttered gridiron, turning it often, as it begins to drip, attempting nothing else while cooking it. Have everything ready for the table; the potatoes and vegetables dished and in the warming closet. Do not season it until it is done, which will be in about ten to twelve minutes. Remove it to a warm platter, pepper and salt it on both sides and spread a liberal lump of butter over it. Serve at once while hot. No definite rule can be given as to the *time* of cooking steak, individual tastes differ so widely in regard to it, some only liking it when well done, others so rare that the blood runs out of it. The best pieces for broiling are the porterhouse and sirloin.

DR. STOWERS

CHIROPODIST AND MASSEUR

Ladies' Shoe Shining Parlor attached.

ROOM 2 MALTA BUILDING
NO. 11 WEST FIFTH ST.   CINCINNATI, O.

TELEPHONE MAIN 3389-X

STEWED BRISKET OF BEEF.

Put the part that has the hard fat into a stewpot with a small quantity of water; let it boil up and skim it thoroughly; then add carrots, turnips, onions, celery and a few pepper-corns. Stew till extremely tender; then take out all the flat bones and remove all the fat from the soup. Either serve that and the meat in a tureen, or the soup alone, and the meat on a dish garnished with some vegetables. The following sauce is much admired served with the beef: Take half a pint of soup and mix it with a spoonful of catsup, a teaspoonful of made mustard, a little flour, a bit of butter and salt; boil all together a few minutes, then pour it round the meat.

BEEF CROQUETTES.

Chop fine one cup of cold, cooked, lean beef, half a cup of fat, half a cup of cold boiled or fried ham; cold pork will do if you have not the ham. Also mince up a slice of onion. Season all with a teaspoonful of salt, half a teaspoonful of pepper, and a teaspoonful of powdered sage or parsley if liked. Heat together with half a cup of stock or milk; when cool add a beaten egg. Form the mixture into balls, slightly flattened, roll in egg and bread crumbs, or flour and egg. Fry in hot lard or beef drippings. Serve on a platter and garnish with sprigs of parsley. Almost any cold meats can be used instead of beef.

SWEETBREADS.

There are two in a calf, which are considered delicacies. Select the largest. The color should be clear and a shade darker than the fat. Before cooking in any manner let them lie for half an hour in tepid water; then throw into hot water to whiten and harden, after which draw off the outer casing, remove the little pipes, and cut into thin slices. They should always be thoroughly cooked.

TYLER—DAVIDSON FOUNTAIN, CINCINNATI

POT ROAST.

This is an old fashioned dish, often cooked in our grandmothers' time.   Take a piece of fresh beef weighing about five or six pounds.   It must not be *too fat*.   Wash it and put it into a pot with barely sufficient water to cover it.   Set it over a slow fire, and after it has stewed an hour salt and pepper it.   Then stew it slowly until tender, adding a little onion if liked.   Do not replenish the water at the last, but let all nearly boil away.   When tender all through take the meat from the pot and pour the gravy in a bowl.   Put a large lump of butter in the bottom of the pot, then dredge the piece of meat with flour and return it to the pot to brown, turning it often to prevent its burning.   Take the gravy that you have poured from the meat into the bowl and skim off all the fat; pour this gravy in with the meat and stir in a large spoonful of flour; wet with a little water; let it boil ten or fifteen minutes and pour into a gravy dish.   Serve both hot, the meat on a platter.   Some are very fond of this way of cooking a piece of beef which has been previously placed in spiced pickle for two or three days.

DRIED BEEF WITH CREAM.

Shave your beef *very* fine.   Put it into a suitable dish on the back of the stove; cover with cold water and give it time to soak out to its original size before being dried.   When it is quite soft and the water has become hot (it must not boil) take it off, turn off the water, pour on a cup of cream; if you do not have it use milk or butter, a pinch of pepper; let it come to a boil, thicken with a table-spoonful of flour wet in a little milk.   Serve on dipped toast or not, just as one fancies.   A nice breakfast dish.

FLANK STEAK.

This is cut from the boneless part of the flank and is secreted between an outside and inside layer of creamy fat.   There are two ways of broiling it.   One is to slice it diagonally across the grain; the other is to broil it whole.   In either case brush butter over it and proceed as in broiling other steaks.   It is considered by butchers the finest steak, which they frequently reserve for themselves.

MRS. FREDERICK H. ALMS.
One of Cincinnati's Benefactors.

HAMBURGER STEAK.

Take a pound of raw flank or round steak, without any fat, bone or stringy pieces. Chop it until a perfect mince; it cannot be chopped to fine. Also chop a little onion quite fine and mix well with the meat. Season with salt and pepper; make into cakes as large as a biscuit, but quite flat, or into one large flat cake a little less than half an inch thick. Have ready a frying pan with butter and lard mixed; when boiling hot put in the steak and fry brown. Garnish with celery top around the edge of the platter and two or three slices of lemon on the top of the meat.

A brown gravy made from the grease the steak was fried in and poured over the meat enriches it.

ROAST LOIN OF VEAL.

Prepare it the same as any roast, leaving in the kidney, around which put considerable salt. Make a dressing the same as for fowls; unroll the loin, put the stuffing well around the kidney, fold and secure with several coils of white cotton twine wound around in all directions; place in a dripping-pan with the thick side down, and put in a rather hot oven, graduated after it commences to roast to moderate; in half an hour add a little hot water to the pan, and baste often; in another half hour turn over the roast, and when about done dredge lightly with flour and baste with melted butter. Before serving, carefully remove the twine. A roast of four to five pounds will bake in about two hours. For a gravy, skim off some of the fat if there is too much in the drippings; dredge in some flour, stir until brown, add some hot water if necessary; boil a few minutes, stir in such sweet herbs as fancied, and put in a gravy boat. Serve with green peas and lemon jelly. Is very nice sliced cold for lunch, and Worcestershire or Chili sauce forms a fine relish.

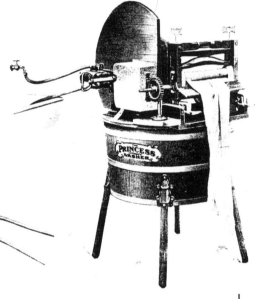

FRIED VEAL CUTLET.

Put into a frying pan two or three tablespoonfuls of lard or beef drippings. When boiling hot lay in the cutlets, well seasoned with salt and pepper and dredged with flour. Brown nicely on both sides, then remove the meat, and if you have more grease than is necessary for the gravy put it aside for further use. Reserve a tablespoonful or more and rub into it a tablespoonful of flour, with the back of spoon, until it is a smooth, rich brown color; then add gradually a cup of *cold water* and season with pepper and salt. When the gravy is boiled up well return the meat to the pan and gravy. Cover it closely and allow it to stew gently on the back of the range for fifteen minutes. This softens the meat, and with this gravy it makes a nice breakfast dish.

Another mode is to simply fry the cutlets, and afterwards turning off some of the grease they were fried in and then adding to that left in the pan a few drops of hot water, turning the whole over the fried chops.

ROAST MUTTON.

The pieces mostly used for roasting are the hind-quarter of the sheep, called the loin and leg, the fore-quarter, the shoulder, also the chine or saddle, which is the two loins together. Every part should be trimmed off that cannot be eaten; then wash well and dry with a clean cloth; lay it in your dripping-pan and put in a little water to baste it with at first; then afterwards with its own gravy. Allow, in roasting, about twelve minutes to the pound; that is, if your fire is strong, which it should be. It should not be salted at first, as that tends to harden it, and draws out too much of the blood or juices; but salt soon after it begins to roast well. If there is danger of its browning too fast, cover it with a sheet of white paper. Baste it often, and about a quarter of an hour before you think it will be done, dredge the meat very lightly with flour and baste it with butter. Skim the gravy well and thicken very slightly with brown flour. Serve with currant jelly or other tart sauce.

VEAL POT-PIE.

Procure a nice breast or brisket of veal, well jointed, put the pieces into a pot with one quart of water to every five pounds of meat; put the pot over a slow fire; just before it comes to a boil, skim it well and pour in a teacupful of cold water; then turn over the meat in order that the scum may rise; remove all the scum, boil quite hard, season with pepper and salt to your taste, always re membering that the crust will take up part of the seasoning; when this is done cut off your crust in pieces of equal size, but do not roll or mould them; lay them on top of the meat, so as to cover it; put the lid on the pot closely, let the whole boil slowly one hour. If the lid does not fit the pot closely, wrap a cloth around it, in order that do steam shall escape; and by no means allow the pot to *stop boiling*.

CROQUETTES OF SWEETBREADS.

Take four veal sweetbreads, soak them for an hour in cold salted water; first remove the pipes and membranes; then put them into boiling salted water with a tablespoonful of vinegar, and cook them twenty minutes, then drop them again into cold water to harden. Now remove them, chop them very fine, almost to a paste. Season with salt, pepper and a tabespoonful of grated onion; add the beaten yolks of three raw eggs, one tablespoonful of butter, half a cupful of cream, and sufficient fine cracker crumbs to make stiff enough to roll out into little balls or cork-shaped croquettes. Have ready a frying kettle half full of fat over the fire, a dish containing three smoothly beaten eggs, a large platter of cracker dust; wet the hands with cold water and make the mixture in shape; afterwards rolling them in the cracker dust, then into the beaten egg, and again in the cracker dust; smooth them on the outside and drop them carefully in the hot fat. When the croquettes are fried a nice golden brown, put them on a brown paper a moment to free them from grease. Serve hot with sliced lemon or parsley.

ONIONS BOILED.

The white silver-skins are the best species. To boil them peel off the outside, cut off the ends, put them into cold water and into a stewpan and let them scald two minutes; then turn off that water, pour on cold water salted a little, and boil slowly till tender, which will be in thirty or forty minutes, according to their size; when done drain them quite dry, pour a little melted butter over them, sprinkle them with pepper and salt and serve hot.

An excellent way to peel onions so as not to affect the eyes is to take a pan *full* of water and hold and peel them under the water.

ONIONS STEWED.

Cook the same as boiled onions, and, when quite done, turn off all the water; add a teacupful of milk, a piece of butter the size of an egg, pepper and salt to taste, a tablespoonful of flour stirred to a cream; let all boil up once and serve in a vegetable dish hot.

FRIED ONIONS.

Peel, slice and fry them brown in equal quantities of butter and lard or nice drippings, cover until partly soft, remove the cover and brown them, salt and pepper.

TO BOIL RICE.

Pick over the rice carefully, wash it in warm water, rubbing it between the hands, rinsing it in several waters, then let it remain in cold water until ready to be cooked. Have a saucepan of water slightly salted; when it is boiling hard, pour off the cold water from the rice, and sprinkle it in the boiling water by degrees, so as to keep the particles separated. Boil it steadily for twenty minutes, then take it off from the fire and drain off all the water. Place the saucepan with the lid partly off, on the back part of the stove, where it is only moderately warm, to allow the rice to dry. The moisture will pass off and each grain of rice will be separated, so that if shaken the grains will fall apart. This is the true way of serving rice as a vegetable and is the mode of cooking it in the Southern States where it is raised.

BOILED CABBAGE.

Great care is requisite in cleaning a cabbage for boiling, as it frequently harbors insects. The large drumhead cabbage requires an hour to boil; the green savory cabbage will boil in twenty minutes. Add considerable salt to the water when boiling. Do not let a cabbage boil too long—by a long boiling it becomes watery. Remove it from the water into a colander to drain and serve with drawn butter, or butter poured over it.

Red cabbage is used for slaw, as is also the white winter cabbage. For directions to prepare these varieties, see articles Slaw and Sourcrout.

CABBAGE with CREAM.

Remove the outer leaves from a solid, small-sized head of cabbage, and cut the remainder as fine as for slaw. Have on the fire a spider or deep skillet, and when it is hot put in the cut cabbage, pouring over it right away a pint of boiling water. Cover closely and allow it to cook rapidly for ten minutes. Drain off the water and add half a pint of new milk, or part milk and cream; when it boils, stir in a large teaspoonful of either wheat or rice flour moistened with milk; add salt and pepper, and as soon as it comes to a boil, serve. Those who find slaw and other dishes prepared from cabbage indigestible will not complain of this.

STEWED PARSNIPS.

After washing and scraping the parsnips slice them about half an inch thick. Put them in a saucepan of boiling water containing just enough to barely cook them; add a tablespoonful of butter, season with salt and pepper, then cover closely. Stew them until the water has cooked away, washing carefully and stirring often to prevent burning, until they are soft. When they are done they will be of a creamy light straw color and deliciously sweet, retaining all the goodness of the vegetable.

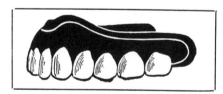

BOILED BEETS.

Select small-sized, smooth. roots. They should be carefully washed, but not cut before boiling, as the juice will escape and the sweetness of the vegetable be impaired, leaving it white and hard. Put them into boiling water, and boil them until tender, which requires often from one to two hours. Do not probe them, but press them with the finger to ascertain if they are sufficiently done. When satisfied of this, take them up, and put them into a pan of cold water, and slip off the outside. Cut them into slices, and while hot season with butter, salt, a little pepper and very sharp vinegar.

GREEN CORN STEWED.

This should be cooked on the same day it is gathered; it loses its sweetness in a few hours and must be artificially supplied. Strip off the husks, pick out all the silk and put it in boiling water; if not entirely fresh, add a tablespoonful of sugar to the water, but *no salt;* boil twenty minutes, fast, and serve; or you may cut it from the cob, put in plenty of butter and a little salt, and serve in a covered vegetable dish. The corn is much sweeter when cooked with the husks on, but requires longer time to boil. Will generally boil in twenty minutes.

Green corn left over from dinner makes a nice breakfast dish, prepared as follows: Cut the corn from the cob, and put into a bowl with a cup of milk to every cup of corn, a half cup of flour, one egg, a pinch of salt, and a little butter. Mix well into a thick batter, and fry in small cakes in very hot butter. Serve with plenty of butter and powdered sugar.

FRIED CORN.

Cut the corn off the cob, taking care not to bring off any of the husk with it and to have the grains as separate as possible. Fry in a little butter—just enough to keep it from sticking to the pan; stir very often. When nicely browned, add salt and pepper and a little rich cream. Do not set it near the stove after the cream is added; as it will be apt to turn. This makes a nice dinner or breakfast dish.

SPINACH.

It should be cooked so as to retain its bright green color and not sent to table, as it so often is, of a dull brown or olive color; to retain its fresh appearance, do not cover the vessel while it is cooking.

Spinach requires close examination and picking, as insects are frequently found among it and it is often gritty. Wash it through three or four waters. Then drain it and put it in boiling water. Fifteen to twenty minutes is generally sufficient time to boil spinach Be careful to remove the scum. When it is quite tender, take it up, and drain and squeeze it well. Chop it fine, and put it into a saucepan with a piece of butter and a little pepper and salt. Set it on the fire and let it stew five minutes, stirring it all the time, until quite dry. Turn it into a vegetable dish, shape it into a mound, slice some hard-boiled eggs and lay around the top.

STEWED CARROTS.

Wash and scrape the carrots and divide them into strips; put them into a stewpan with water enough to cover them; add a spoonful of salt and let them boil slowly until tender; then drain and replace them in the pan, with two tablespoonfuls of butter rolled in flour, shake over a little pepper and salt, then add enough cream or milk to moisten the whole; let it come to a boil and serve hot.

CARROTS MASHED.

Scrape and wash them; cook them tender in boiling water salted slightly. Drain well and mash them. Work in a good piece of butter and season with pepper and salt. Heap up a vegetable dish and serve hot.

Carrots are also good simply boiled in salted water and dished up hot with melted butter over them.

TURNIPS.

Turnips are boiled plain with or without meat, also mashed like potatoes and stewed like parsnips. They should always be served hot. They require from forty minutes to an hour to cook.

STEWED GREEN PEAS.

Into a saucepan of boiling water put two or three pints of young green peas, and when nearly done and tender drain in a colander dry; then melt two ounces of butter in two of flour; stir well and boil five minutes longer; should the pods be quite clean and fresh boil them first in the water, remove and put in the peas. The Germans prepare a very palatable dish of sweet young pods alone by simply stirring in a little butter with some savory herbs.

STEWED PUMPKIN.

See Stewed Pumpkin for Pie. Cook the same, then after stewing season the same as mashed potatoes. Pumpkin is good baked in the same manner as baked winter squash.

STEWED MUSHROOMS.

Time, twenty-one minutes. Button mushrooms, salt to taste, a little butter rolled in flour, two tablespoonfuls of cream or the yolk of one egg. Choose buttons of uniform size. Wipe them clean and white with a wet flannel; put them in a stewpan with a little water and let them stew very gently for a quarter of an hour. Add salt to taste, work in a little flour and butter, to make the liquor about as thick as cream, and let it boil for five minutes. When you are ready to dish it up, stir in two tablespoonfuls of cream or the yolk of one egg; stir it over the fire for a minute, but do not let it boil, and serve. Stewed button mushrooms are very nice, either in fish stews or ragouts, or served apart to eat with fish. Another way of doing them is to stew them in milk and water (after they are rubbed white), add to them a little veal gravy, mace and salt and thicken the gravy with cream or the yolks of eggs.

Mushrooms can be cooked in the same manner as the recipes for oysters, either stewed, fried, broiled, or as a soup. They are also used to flavor sauces, catsups, meat gravies, game and soups.

CORN PUDDING.

This is a Virginia dish. Scrape the substance out of twelve ears of tender, green, uncooked corn (it is better scraped than grated, as you do not get those husky particles which you cannot avoid with a grater); add yolks and whites, beaten separately, of four eggs, a teaspoonful of sugar, the same of flour mixed in a tablespoonful of butter, a small quantity of salt and pepper, and one pint of milk. Bake about half or three-quarters of an hour.

STEWED CORN.

Take a dozen ears of green sweet corn, very tender and juicy; cut off the kernels, cutting with a large sharp knife from the top of the cob down; then scrape the cob. Put the corn into a saucepan over the fire with just enough water to make it cook without burning; boil about twenty minutes, then add a cupful of milk or cream, a tablespoonful of cold butter, and season with pepper and salt. Boil ten minutes longer and dish up hot in a vegetable dish. The corn would be much sweeter if the scraped cobs were boiled first in the water that the corn is cooked in.

Many like corn cooked in this manner, putting half corn and half tomatoes; either way is very good.

SUCCOTASH.

Take a pint of fresh shelled Lima beans, or any large fresh beans, put them in a pot with cold water, rather more than will cover them. Scrape the kernels from twelve ears of young sweet corn; put the cobs in with the beans, boiling from half to three-quarters of an hour. Now take out the cobs and put in the scraped corn; boil again fifteen minutes, then season with salt and pepper to taste, a piece of butter the size of an egg and half a cup of cream. Serve hot.

CELERY.

This is stewed the same as green corn, by boiling, adding cream, butter, salt and pepper.

STEWED BEETS.

Boil them first and then scrape and slice them. Put them into a stewpan with a piece of butter rolled in flour, some boiled onion and parsley chopped fine, and a little vinegar, salt and pepper. Set the pan on the fire, and let the beets stew for a quarter of an hour.

OKRA.

This grows in the shape of pods, and is of a gelatinous character, much used for soup, and is also pickled; it may be boiled as follows: Put the young and tender pods of long white orka in salted boiling water in granite, porcelain or a tin-lined saucepan—as contact with iron will discolor it; boil fifteen minutes; remove the stems, and serve with butter, pepper, salt and vinegar if preferred.

ASPARAGUS.

Scrape the stems of the asparagus lightly, but very clean; throw them into cold water and when they are all scraped and very clean, tie them in bunches of equal size; cut the large ends evenly, that the stems may be all of the same length, and put the asparagus into plenty of boiling water; well salted. While it is boiling, cut several slices of bread half an inch thick, pare off the crust and toast it a delicate brown on both sides. When the stalks of the asparagus are tender (it will usually cook in twenty to forty minutes) lift it out directly, or it will lose both its color and flavor and will also be liable to break; dip the toast quickly into the liquor in which it was boiled and dish the vegetable upon it, the heads all lying one way. Pour over white sauce, or melted butter.

MACARONI and TOMATO SAUCE.

Divide half a pound of macaroni into four-inch pieces, put it into boiling salted water enough to cover it; boil from fifteen to twenty minutes, then drain; arrange it neatly on a hot dish and pour tomato sauce over it, and serve immediately while hot. See Sauces for tomato sauce.

SQUASHES, OR CYMBLINGS.

The green or summer squash is best when the outside is beginning to turn yellow, as it is then less watery and insipid than when younger. Wash them, cut them into pieces and take out the seeds. Boil them about three-quarters of an hour, or till quite tender. When done, drain and squeeze them well till you have pressed out all the water; mash them with a little butter, pepper and salt. Then put the squash thus prepared into a stewpan, set it on hot coals and stir it very frequently till it becomes dry. Take care not to let it burn.

Summer squash is very nice steamed, then prepared the same as boiled.

VEGETABLE HASH.

Chop rather coarsely the remains of vegetables left from a boiled dinner, such as cabbage, parsnips, potatoes, etc.; sprinkle over them a little pepper, place in a saucepan or frying pan over the fire; put in a piece of butter the size of a hickory nut; when it begins to melt, tip the dish so as to oil the bottom and around the sides; then put in the chopped vegetables, pour in a spoonful or two of hot water from the tea-kettle, cover quickly so as to keep in the steam. When heated thoroughly take off the cover and stir occasionally until well cooked. Serve hot. Persons fond of vegetables will relish this dish very much.

GREEN PEAS.

Shell the peas and wash in cold water. Put in boiling water just enough to cover them well and keep them from burning; boil from twenty minutes to half an hour, when the liquor should be nearly boiled out; season with pepper and salt and a good allowance of butter; serve very hot.

This is a very much better way than cooking in a larger quantity of water and draining off the liquor, as that diminishes the sweetness, and much of the fine flavor of the peas is lost. The salt should never be put in the peas before they are tender, unless very young, as it tends to harden them.

STEWED TOMATOES.

Pour boiling water over a dozen sound ripe tomatoes; let them remain for a few moments; then peel off the skins, slice them and put them over the fire in a well-lined tin or granite-ware saucepan. Stew them about twenty minutes, then add a tablespoonful of butter, salt and pepper to taste; let them stew fifteen minutes longer and serve hot. Some prefer to thicken tomatoes with a little grated bread, adding a teaspoonful of sugar; and others who like the flavor of onion chop up one and add while stewing; then again, some add as much green corn as there are tomatoes.

STUFFED BAKED TOMATOES.

From the blossom-end of a dozen tomatoes; smooth, ripe and solid, cut a thin slice and with a small spoon scoop out the pulp without breaking the rind surrounding it; chop a small head of cabbage and a good-sized onion fine and mix with them fine bread crumbs and the pulp; season with pepper, salt and sugar and add a cup of sweet cream; when all is well mixed, fill the tomato shells, replace the slices and place the tomatoes in a buttered baking-dish, cut ends up and put in the pan just enough water to keep from burning; drop a small lump of butter on each tomato and bake half an hour or so, till well done; place another bit of butter on each and serve in same dish. Very fine.

Another stuffing which is considered quite fine. Cut a slice from the stem of each and scoop out the soft pulp. Mince one small onion and fry it slightly; add a gill of hot water, the tomato pulp and two ounces of cold veal or chicken chopped fine, simmer slowly and season with salt and pepper. Stir into the pan cracker dust or bread crumbs enough to absorb the moisture; take off from the fire and let it cool; stuff the tomatoes with this mass, sprinkle dry crumbs over the top; add a small piece of butter to the top of each and bake until slightly browned on top.

FRIED PARSNIPS.

Boil tender in a little hot water salted; scrape, cut into long slices, dredge with flour; fry in hot lard or dripping, or in butter and lard mixed; fry quite brown.   Drain off fat and serve.

Parsnips may be boiled and mashed the same as potatoes.

SOURCROUT.

Barrels having held wine or vinegar are used to prepare sourcrout in.   It is better, however, to have a special barrel for the purpose. Strasburg, as well as all Alsace, has a well-acquired fame for preparing the cabbages.   They slice very white and firm cabbages in fine shreds with a machine made for the purpose.   At the bottom of a small barrel they place a layer of coarse salt and alternately layers of cabbage and salt, being careful to have one of salt on the top.   As each layer of cabbage is added, it must be pressed down by a large and heavy pestle and fresh layers are added as soon as the juice floats on the surface.   The cabbage must be seasoned with a few grains of coriander, juniper berries, etc.   When the barrel is full it must be put in a dry cellar, covered with a cloth, under a plank, and on this heavy weights are placed.   At the end of a few days it will begin to ferment, during which time the pickle must be drawn off and replaced by fresh, until the liquor becomes clear. This should be done everyday.   Renew the cloth and wash the cover, put the weights back and let stand for a month.   By that time the sourcrout will be ready for use.   Care must be taken to let the least possible air enter the sourcrout and to have the cover perfectly clean.   Each time the barrel has to be opened it must be properly closed again.   These precautions must not be neglected.

This is often fried in the same manner as fried cabbage, excepting it is first boiled until soft in just water enough to cook it, then fry and add vinegar.

SARATOGA CHIPS.

Peel good-sized potatoes, and slice them as evenly as possible. Drop them into ice-water; have a kettle of very hot lard, as for cakes; put a few at a time into a towel and shake, to dry the moisture out of them, and then drop them into the boiling lard. Stir them occasionally, and when of a light brown take them out with a skimmer, and they will be crisp and not greasy. Sprinkle salt over them while hot.

FRIED RAW POTATOES.

Peel half a dozen medium-sized potatoes very evenly, cut them in slices as thin as an egg-shell, and be sure to cut them from the *breadth*, not the length, of the potato. Put a tablespoonful each of butter and sweet lard into the frying pan, and as soon as it boils add the sliced potatoes, sprinkling over them salt and pepper to season them. Cover them with a tight-fitting lid, and let the steam partly cook them; then remove it, and let them fry a bright gold color, shaking and turning them carefully, so as to brown equally. Serve very hot.

Fried, cold cooked potatoes may be fried by the same recipe, only slice them a little thicker.

Remark.—Boiled or steamed potatoes chopped up or sliced while they are yet warm never fry so successfully as when cold.

LYONNAISE POTATOES.

Take eight or ten good-sized cold boiled potatoes, slice them endwise, then crosswise, making them like dice in small squares. When you are ready to cook them, heat some butter or good drippings in a frying pan; fry in it one small onion (chopped fine) until it begins to change color and look yellow. Now put in your potatoes, sprinkle well with salt and pepper, stir well and cook about five minutes, taking care that you do not break them. *They must not brown*. Just before taking up stir in a tablespoonful of minced parsley. Drain dry by shaking in a heated colander. Serve *very hot*.

POTATO CROQUETTES.

Wash, peel and put four large potatoes in cold water, with a pinch of salt, and set them over a brisk fire; when they are done pour off all the water and mash them. Take another saucepan, and put in it ten tablespoonfuls of milk and a lump of butter half the size of an egg; put it over a brisk fire; as soon as the milk comes to a boil, pour the potatoes into it, and stir them very fast with a wooden spoon; when thoroughly mixed, take them from the fire and put them on a dish. Take a tablespoonful and roll it in a clean towel, making it oval in shape; dip it in a well-beaten egg, and then in bread crumbs, and drop it in hot drippings or lard. Proceed in this manner till all the potato is used, four potatoes make six croquettes. Fry them a light brown all over, turning them gently as may be necessary. When they are done, lay them on brown paper or a hair sieve, to drain off all fat; then serve on a napkin.

BAKED POTATOES.

Potatoes are either baked in their jackets or peeled; in either case they should not be exposed to a fierce heat which is wasteful, inasmuch as thereby a great deal of vegetable is scorched and rendered uneatable. They should be frequently turned while being baked and kept from touching each other in the oven or dish. When done in their skins, be particular to wash and brush them before baking them. If convenient, they may be baked in wood-ashes, or in a Dutch oven in front of the fire. When pared they should be baked in a dish and fat of some kind added to prevent their outsides from becoming burnt, they are ordinarily baked thus as an accessory to baked meat.

Never serve potatoes, boiled or baked whole, in a closely covered dish. They become sodden and clammy. Cover with a folded napkin that allows the steam to escape, or absorbs the moisture. They should be served promptly when done and require about three-quarters of an hour to one hour to bake them if of a good size.

MASHED POTATOES.

Take the quantity needed, pare off the skins and lay them in cold water half an hour; then put them into a saucepan with a little salt; cover with water and boil them until done. Drain off the water and mash them fine with a potato masher. Have ready a piece of butter the size of an egg melted in half a cup of boiling hot milk and a good pinch of salt; mix it well with the mashed potatoes until they are a smooth paste, taking care that they are not too wet. Put them into a vegetable dish, heap them up and smooth over the top, put a small piece of butter on the top in the centre, and have dots of pepper here and there on the surface as large as a half dime.

Some prefer using a heavy fork or wire beater, instead of a potato masher, beating the potatoes quite light and heaping them up in the dish without smoothing over the top.

BAKED SWEET POTATOES.

Wash and scrape them, split them lengthwise. Steam or boil them until nearly done. Drain, and put them in a baking dish, placing over them lumps of butter, pepper and salt; sprinkle thickly with sugar, and bake in the oven to a nice brown.

Hubbard squash is nice cooked in the same manner.

CAULIFLOWER.

When cleaned and washed, drop them into boiling water, into which you have put salt and a teaspoonful of flour, or a slice of bread, boil till tender, take off, drain and dish them, serve with a sauce spread over and made with melted butter, salt, pepper, grated nutmeg, chopped parsley and vinegar.

Another way is to make a white sauce (see Sauces) and when the cauliflowers are dished as above, turn the white sauce over, and serve warm. They may also be served in the same way with a milk, cream or tomato sauce, or with brown butter.

It is a very good plan to loosen the leaves of a head of cauliflower and let lie, the top downward, in a pan of cold salt water, to remove any insects that might be hidden between them.

TO BOIL NEW POTATOES.

Do not have the potatoes dug long before they are dressed, as they are never good after they have been out of the ground for some time. Well wash them, rub off the skins with a coarse cloth, and put them in *boiling* water salted. Let them boil until tender; try them with a fork, and when done pour the water away from them; let them stand by the side of the fire with the lid of the saucepan partially removed, and when the potatoes are thoroughly dry, put them in a hot vegetable dish, with a piece of butter the size of a walnut; pile the potatoes over this and serve. If the potatoes are too old to have the skins rubbed off; boil them in their jackets; drain, peel and serve them as above, with a piece of butter in the midst of them. They require twenty to thirty minutes to cook. Serve them hot and plain or with melted butter over them.

BROWNED POTATOES with a ROAST.

About three-quarters of an hour before taking up your roasts, peel middling-sized potatoes, boil them until partly done, then arrange them in the roasting-pan around the roast, basting them with the drippings at the same time you do the meat, browning them evenly. Serve hot with the meat. Many cooks partly boil the potatoes before putting around the roast. New potatoes are very good cooked a-round a roast.

BROWNED POTATOES.

Mash them the same as the above, put them into a dish that they are to be served in, smooth over the top and brush over with the yolk of an egg, or spread on a bountiful supply of butter and dust well with flour. Set it in the oven to brown; it will brown in fifteen minutes with a quick fire.

POTATOES A LA CREME.

Heat a cupful of milk; stir in a heaping tablespoonful of butter cut up in as much flour. Stir until smooth and thick; pepper and salt, and add two cupfuls of cold boiled potatoes, sliced, and a little very finely chopped parsley. Shake over the fire until the potatoes are hot all through, and pour into a deep dish.

FRIED EGG-PLANT.

Take fresh, purple egg-plants of a middling size; cut them in slices a quarter of an inch thick, and soak them for half an hour in cold water, with a teaspoonful of salt in it. Have ready some cracker or bread crumbs and one beaten egg; drain off the water from the slices, lay them on a napkin, dip them in the crumbs and then in the egg, put another coat of crumbs on them and fry them in butter to a light brown. The frying pan must be hot before the slices are put in—they will fry in ten minutes.

You may pare them before you put them into the frying pan, or you may pull off the skins when you take them up. You must not remove them from the water until you are ready to cook them, as the air will turn them black.

STUFFED EGG-PLANT.

Cut the egg-plant in two; scrape out all the inside and put it in a saucepan with a little minced ham; cover with water and boil until soft; drain off the water; add two tablespoonfuls of grated crumbs, a tablespoonful of butter, half a minced onion, salt and pepper; stuff each half of the hull with the mixture; add a small lump of butter to each and bake fifteen minutes. Minced veal or chicken in the place of ham, is equally as good and many prefer it.

STRING BEANS.

Break off the end that grew to the vine, drawing off at the same time the string upon the edge; repeat the same process from the other end; cut them with a sharp knife into pieces half an inch long, and boil them in *just enough* water to *cover* them. They usually require one hour's boiling; but this depends upon their age and freshness. After they have boiled until tender and the water *boiled nearly out*, add pepper and salt, a tablespoonful of butter and a half a cup of cream; if you have not the cream add more butter.

Many prefer to drain them before adding the seasoning; in that case they lose the real goodness of the vegetable.

BOILED EGGS.

Eggs for boiling cannot be too fresh, or boiled too soon after they are laid; but rather a longer time should be allowed for boiling a new-laid egg than for one that is three or four days old. Have ready a saucepan of boiling water; put the eggs into it gently with a spoon, letting the spoon touch the bottom of the saucepan before it is withdrawn, that the egg may not fall and consequently crack. For those who like eggs lightly boiled, three minutes will be found sufficient; three and three-quarters to four minutes will be ample time to set the whites nicely; and if liked hard, six or seven minutes will not be found too long. Should the eggs be unusually large, as those of black Spanish fowls sometimes are, allow an extra half minute for them. Eggs for salad should be boiled for ten or fifteen minutes, and should be placed in a basin of cold water for a few minutes to shrink the meat from the shell; they should then be rolled on the table with the hand and the shell will peel off easily.

SOFT BOILED EGGS.

When properly cooked eggs are done evenly through, like any other food. This result may be obtained by putting the eggs into a dish with a cover, or a tin pail, and then pouring upon them *boiling* water—two quarts or more to a dozen of eggs—and cover and set them away where they will keep *hot* and *not* boil for ten to twelve minutes. The heat of the water cooks the eggs slowly, evenly and sufficiently, leaving the centre or yolk harder than the white.

SCALLOPED EGGS.

Hard-boil twelve eggs; slice them thin in rings; in the bottom of a large well-buttered baking-dish place a layer of grated bread crumbs, then one of eggs; cover with bits of butter and sprinkle with pepper and salt. Continue thus to blend these ingredients until the dish is full; be sure, though, that the crumbs cover the eggs upon top. Over the whole pour a large teacupful of sweet cream or milk and brown nicely in a moderately heated oven.

SCRAMBLED EGGS.

Put a tablespoonful of butter into a hot frying pan; tip around so that it will touch all sides of the pan. Having ready half a dozen eggs broken in a dish, salted and peppered, turn them (without beating) into the hot butter; stir them one way briskly for five or six minutes or until they are mixed. Be careful that they do not get too hard. Turn over toast or dish up without.

POACHED OR DROPPED EGGS.

Have one quart of *boiling* water and one tablespoonful of salt in a frying pan. Break the eggs, one by one, into a saucer, and slide carefully into the salted water. Dash with a spoon a little water over the egg, to keep the top white.

The beauty of a poached egg is for the yolk to be seen blushing through the white, which should only be just sufficiently hardened to form a transparent veil for the egg.

Cook until the white is firm, and lift out with a griddle cake turner, and place on toasted bread. Serve immediately.

A tablespoonful of vinegar put into the water keeps the eggs from spreading.

Open gem rings are nice placed in the water and an egg dropped into each ring.

FRIED EGGS.

Break the eggs, one at a time, into a saucer, and then slide them carefully off into a frying pan of lard and butter mixed, dipping over the eggs the hot grease in spoonfuls, or turn them over, frying both sides without breaking them. They require about three minutes' cooking.

Eggs can be fried round like balls, by dropping one at a time into a quantity of hot lard, the same as for fried cakes, first stirring the hot lard with a stick until it runs round like a whirlpool; this will make the eggs look like balls. Take out with a skimmer. Eggs can be poached the same in boiling water

CHICKEN OMELET.

Mince rather fine one cupful of cooked chicken, warm in a tea-cupful of cream or rich milk, a tablespoonful of butter, salt and pepper; thicken with a large tablespoonful of flour. Make a plain omelet, then add this mixture just before turning it over. This is much better than the dry minced chicken. Tongue is equally good.

OYSTER OMELET.

Parboil a dozen oysters in their own liquor, skim them out and let them cool; add them to the beaten eggs, either whole or minced. Cook the same as a plain omelet.

Thicken the liquid with butter rolled in flour; season with salt, cayenne pepper and a teaspoonful of chopped parsley. Chop up the oysters and add to the sauce. Put a few spoonfuls in the centre of the omelet before folding; when dished, pour the remainder of the sauce around it.

PLAIN OMELETS.

Put a smooth, clean, iron frying pan on the fire to heat; meanwhile, beat four eggs very light, the whites to a stiff froth and the yolks to a thick batter. Add to the yolks four tablespoonfuls cf milk, pepper and salt; and, lastly, stir in the whites lightly. Put a piece of butter nearly half the size of an egg into the heated pan; turn it so that it will moisten the entire bottom, taking care that it does not scorch. Just as it begins to boil, pour in the eggs. Hold the frying pan handle in your left hand, and, as the eggs whiten, carefully, with a spoon, draw up lightly from the bottom, letting the raw part run out on the pan, till all be equally cooked; shake with your left hand, till the omelet be free from the pan, then turn with a spoon one half of the omelet over the other; let it remain a moment, but continue shaking, lest it adhere; toss to a warm platter held in the right hand, or lift with a flat, broad shovel; the omelet will be firm around the edge, but creamy and light inside.

OMELETS.

In making an omelet, care should be taken that the omelet pan is hot and dry. To ensure this, put a small quantity of lard or suet into a clean frying pan, let it simmer a few minutes, then remove it; wipe the pan dry with a towel, and then put in a tablespoonful of butter. The smoothness of the pan is most essential, as the least particle of roughness will cause the omelet to stick. As a general rule, a small omelet can be made more successfully than a large one, it being much better to make two small ones of four eggs each, than to try double the number of eggs in one omelet and fail. Allow one egg to a person in making an omelet and one tablespoonful of milk; this makes an omelet more puffy and tender than one made without milk. Many prefer them without milk.

Omelets are called by the name of what is added to give them flavor, as minced ham, salmon, onions, oysters, etc., beaten up in the eggs in due quantity, which gives as many different kinds of omelets.

They are also served over many kinds of thick sauces or purees, such as tomatoes, spinach, endive, lettuce, celery, etc.

If vegetables are to be added, they should be already cooked, seasoned and hot; place in the centre of the omelet, just before turning; so with mushroom, shrimps, or any cooked ingredients. All omelets should be served the moment they are done, as they harden by standing, and care taken that they do not *cook too much*.

Sweet omelets are generally used for breakfast or plain desserts.

BAKED OMELET.

Beat the whites and yolks of four or six eggs separately; add to the yolks a small cup of milk, a tablespoonful of flour or cornstarch, a teaspoonful of baking powder, one-half teaspoonful of salt, and, lastly, the stiff-beaten whites. Bake in a well buttered pie-tin or plate about half an hour in a steady oven. It should be served the moment it is taken from the oven, as it is liable to fall.

RUM OMELET.

Put a small quantity of lard into the pan; let it simmer a few minutes and remove it; wipe the pan dry with a towel, and put in a little fresh lard in which the omelet may be fried. Care should be taken that the lard does not burn, which would spoil the color of the omelet. Break three eggs separately; put them into a bowl and whisk them thoroughly with a fork. The longer they are beaten, the lighter will the omelet be. Beat up a teaspoonful of milk with the eggs and continue to beat until the last moment before pouring into the pan, which should be over a hot fire. As soon as the omelet sets, remove the pan from the hottest part of the fire. Slip a knife under it to prevent sticking to the pan. When the centre is almost firm, slant the pan, work the omelet in shape to fold easily and neatly, and when slightly browned, hold a platter against the edge of the pan and deftly turn it out on to the hot dish. Dust a liberal quantity of powdered sugar over it, and singe the sugar into neat stripes with hot iron rod, heated in the coals; pour a glass of warm Jamaica rum around it, and when it is placed on the table set fire to the rum. With a tablespoon dash the burning rum over the omelet, put out the fire and serve. Salt *mixed* with the eggs prevents them from rising, and when it is so used the omelet will look flabby, yet without salt it will taste insipid. Add a little salt to it just before folding it and turning out on a dish.

TOMATO OMELET.

Peel a couple of tomatoes, which split into four pieces; remove the seeds and cut them into small dice; then fry them with a little butter until nearly done, added salt and pepper. Beat the eggs and mix the tomatoes with them, and make the omelet as usual. Or stew a few tomatoes in the usual way and spread over before folding.

JELLY OMELET.

Make a plain omelet, and just before folding together, spread with some kind of jelly. Turn out on a warm platter. Dust it with powdered sugar.

PAN-FISH.

Place them in a thick bottomed frying pan with heads all one way. Fill the spaces with smaller fish. When they are fried quite brown and ready to turn, put a dinner plate over them, drain off the fat; then invert the pan, and they will be left unbroken on the plate. Put the lard back into the pan, and when *hot* slip back the fish. When the other side is brown, drain, turn on a plate as before, and slip them on a warm platter, to be sent to the table. Leaving the heads on and the fish a crispy-brown, in perfect shape, improves the appearance if not the flavor. Garnish with slices of lemon.

BAKED WHITE FISH.

Thoroughly clean the fish; cut off the head or not, as preferred; cut out the backbone from the head to within two inches of the tail, and stuff with the following: Soak stale bread in water, squeeze dry; cut in pieces a large onion, fry in butter, chop fine; add the bread, two ounces of butter, salt, pepper and a little parsley or sage; heat through, and when taken off the fire, add the yolks of two well-beaten eggs; stuff the fish rather full, sew up with fine twine, and wrap with several coils of white tape. Rub the fish over slightly with butter; just cover the bottom of the baking pan with hot water, and place the fish in it, standing back upward, and bent in the form of an S. Serve with the following dressing: Reduce the yolks of two hard-boiled eggs to a smooth paste with two tablespoonfuls good salad oil; stir in half a teaspoon English mustard, and add pepper and vinegar to taste.

BAKED WHITE FISH (Bordeaux Sauce.)

Clean and stuff the fish. Put it in a baking-pan and add a liberal quantity of butter, previously rolled in flour, to the fish. Put in the pan half a pint of claret, and bake for an hour and a quarter. Remove the fish and strain the gravy; add to the latter a gill more of claret, a teaspoonful of brown flour and a pinch of cayenne, and serve with the fish.

FRESH SALMON FRIED.

Cut the slices three-quarters of an inch thick, dredge them with flour, or dip them in egg and crumbs, fry a light brown. This mode answers for all fish cut into steaks. Season well with pepper and salt.

BOILED SALT MACKEREL.

Wash and clean off all the brine and salt; put it to soak with the meat side down, in cold water over night; in the morning rinse it in one or two waters. Wrap each up in a cloth and put it into a kettle with considerable water, which should be cold; cook about thirty minutes. Take it carefully from the cloth, take out the backbones and pour over a little melted butter and cream; add a light sprinkle of pepper. Or make a cream sauce like the following:

Heat a small cup of milk to scalding. Stir into it a teaspoonful of cornstarch wet up with a little water. When this thickens, add two tablespoonfuls of butter, pepper, salt and chopped parsley, to taste. Beat an egg light, pour the sauce gradually over it, put the mixture again over the fire, and stir one minute, not more.
Pour upon the fish, and serve it with some slices of lemon, or a few sprigs of parsley or water-cress, on the dish as a garnish.

CODFISH BALLS.

Take a pint bowl of codfish picked very fine, two pint bowls of whole raw peeled potatoes, sliced thickly; put them together in plenty of cold water and boil until the potatoes are thoroughly cooked; remove from the fire and drain off all the water. Mash them with the potato masher, add a piece of butter the size of an egg, one well-beaten egg, and three spoonfuls of cream or rich milk. Flour your hands and make into balls or cakes. Put an ounce each of butter and lard into a frying pan; when hot, put in the balls and fry a nice brown. Do not freshen the fish before boiling with the potatoes. Many cooks fry them in a quantity of lard similar to boiled dough-nuts.

FRIED OYSTERS.

Take large oysters from their own liquor into a thickly folded napkin to dry them; then make hot an ounce each of butter and lard in a thick-bottomed frying pan. Season the oysters with pepper and salt, then dip each one into egg and cracker crumbs rolled fine, until it will take up no more. Place them in hot grease and fry them a delicate brown, turning them on both sides by slididg a broad-bladed knife under them. Serve them crisp and hot.

Some prefer to roll oysters in corn meal and others use flour, but they are much more crisp with egg and cracker crumbs.

STEWED OYSTERS.

Drain the liquor from two quarts of oysters; mix with it a small teacupful of hot water, add a little salt and pepper and set it over the fire in a saucepan. Let it boil up once, put in the oysters, let them come to a boil, and when they "ruffle" add two tablespoonfuls of butter. The instant it is melted and well stirred in, put in a pint of boiling milk and take the saucepan from the fire. Serve with oyster or cream crackers while hot.

If thickening is preferred, stir in a little flour or two tablespoonfuls of cracker crumbs.

SCALLOPED OYSTERS.

Have ready about a pint bowl of cracker crumbs. Butter a deep earthen dish; put a layer of the cracker crumbs on the bottom; wet this with some of the oyster liquor; next have a layer of oysters; sprinkle with salt and pepper, and lay small pieces of butter upon them; then another layer of cracker crumbs and oyster juice; then oysters, pepper, salt and butter, and so on, until the dish is full, the top layer to be cracker crumbs. Beat up an egg in a cup of milk and turn over all. Cover the dish and set it in the oven for thirty or forty-five minutes. When baked through, uncover the top, set on the upper grate and brown.

ROAST TURKEY.

Select a young turkey; remove all the feathers carefully, singe it over a burning newspaper on the top of the stove; then "draw" it nicely, being very carefull not to break any of the internal organs; remove the crop carefully; cut off the head, and tie the neck close to the body by drawing the skin over it. Now rinse the inside of the turkey out with several waters, and in the next to the last, mix a teaspoonful of baking soda; oftentimes the inside of a fowl is very sour, especially if it is not freshly killed. Soda, being cleansing, acts as a corrective, and destroys that unpleasant taste which we frequently experience in the dressing when fowls have been killed for some time. Now, after washing, wipe the turkey dry, inside and out, with a clean cloth, rub the inside with some salt, then stuff the breast and body with "Dressing for Fowls." Then sew up the turkey with a strong thread, tie the legs and wings to the body, rub it over with a little soft butter, sprinkle over some salt and pepper, dredge with a little flour; place it in a dripping-pan, pour in a cup of boiling water, and set in the oven. Baste the turkey often turning it around occasionally so that every part will be uniformly baked. When pierced with a fork and the liquid runs out perfectly clear, the bird is done. If any part is likely to scorch, pin over it a piece of buttered white paper. A fifteen pound turkey requires between three and four hours to bake. Serve with cranberry sauce.

Gravy for Turkey.—When you put the turkey into roast, put the neck, heart, liver and gizzard into a stewpan with a pint of water; boil until they become quite tender; take them out of the water, chop the heart and gizzard, mash the liver and throw away the neck; return the chopped heart, gizzard and liver to the liquor in which they were stewed; set it to one side, and when the turkey is done it should be added to the gravy that dripped from the turkey, having first skimmed off the fat from the surface of the dripping-pan; set it all over the fire, boil three minutes and thicken with flour. It will not need brown flour to color the gravy. The garnishes for turkey or chicken are fried oysters, thin slices of ham, slices of lemon, fried sausages, or force meat balls, also parsley.

ROAST GOOSE.

The goose should not be more than eight months old, and the fatter the more tender and juicy the meat. Stuff with the following mixture: Three pints of bread crumbs, six ounces of butter, or part butter and part salt pork, one teaspoonful each of sage, black pepper and salt, one chopped onion. Do not stuff very full, and stitch openings firmly together to keep the flavor in and the fat out. Place in the baking pan with a little water, and baste frequently with salt and water (some add vinegar); turn often so that the sides and back may be nicely browned. Bake two hours or more; when done take from the pan, pour off the fat, and to the brown gravy left add the chopped giblets which have previously been stewed until tender, together with the water they were boiled in; thicken with a little flour and butter rubbed together, bring to a boil and serve. English style.

DRESSING OR STUFFING FOR FOWLS.

For an eight or ten pound turkey, cut the brown crust from slices or pieces of stale bread until you have as much as the inside of a pound loaf; put it into a suitable dish and pour tepid water (not warm, for that makes it heavy) over it; let it stand one minute, as it soaks very quickly. Now take up a handful at a time and squeeze it hard and dry with both hands, placing it, as you go along, in another dish; this process makes it very light. When all is pressed dry, toss it all up lightly through your fingers; now add a teaspoonful each of pepper, salt, powdered savory, sage or the green herb minced fine; add half a cup of melted butter, and a beaten egg, or not. Work thoroughly all together, and it is ready for dressing either fowls, fish or meats. A little chopped sausage in turkey dressing is considered by some an improvement, when well incorporated with the other ingredients. For geese and ducks the stuffing may be made the same as for turkey, with the addition of few slices of onion chopped fine.

OYSTER DRESSING OR STUFFING.

This is made with the same ingredients as the above, with the exception of half a can of oysters drained and slightly chopped and added to the rest. This is used mostly with boiled turkey and chicken, and the remainder of the can of oysters used to make an oyster sauce to be poured over the turkey when served; served generally in a separate dish, to be dipped out as a person desires.

These recipes were obtained from famous cooks for fine dressings of fowls, fish and meats, and their advice was, *always* soak stale bread in *cold* liquid, either milk or water, when *used* for stuffings or puddings, as they were much lighter, hot liquid makes them heavy.

ROAST CHICKEN.

Pick and draw them, wash out well in two or three waters, adding a little soda to the last but one to sweeten it, if there is doubt as to its being fresh. Dry it well with a clean cloth, and fill the crop and body with a stuffing the same as "Dressing for Fowls." Lay it in a dripping-pan, put a pint of hot water and a piece of butter in the dripping-pan, add to it a small tablespoonful of salt, and a small tea spoonful of pepper; baste frequently, and let it roast quickly, without scorching; when nearly done, put a piece of butter the size of a large egg to the water in the pan; when it melts, baste with it, dredge a little flour over, baste again, and let it finish; half an hour will roast a full-grown chicken, if the fire is right. When done, take it up.

Having stewed the necks, gizzards, livers and hearts in a very little water, strain it and mix it hot with the gravy that has dripped from the fowls, and which must be first skimmed. Thicken it with a little browned flour, add to it the livers, hearts and gizzards chopped small. Or, put the giblets in the pan with the chicken and let them roast. Send the fowls to the table with the gravy in a boat. Cranberry sauce should accompany them, or any tart sauce.

ROAST HARE OR RABBIT.

A very close relationship exists between the hare and the rabbit, the chief difference being in the smaller size and shorter legs and ears of the latter. The manner of dressing and preparing each for the table is, therefore, pretty nearly the same. To prepare them for roasting, first skin, wash well in cold water and rinse thoroughly in lukewarm water. If a little musty from being emptied before they were hung up, and afterward neglected, rub the insides with vinegar and afterward remove all taint of the acid by a thorough washing in lukewarm water. After being well wiped with a soft cloth put in a dressing as usual, sew the animal up, truss it, and roast for half or three-quarters of an hour, until well browned, basing it constantly with butter and dredging with flour, just before taking up.

To make a gravy after the rabbits are roasted, pour nearly all the fat out of the pan, but do not pour the bottom or brown part of the drippings; put the pan over the fire, stir into it a heaping tablespoonful of flour, and stir until the flour browns. Then stir in a pint of boiling water. Season the gravy with salt and pepper; let it boil for a moment. Send hot to the table in a tureen with hot rabbit. Serve with currant jelly.

FRIED RABBIT.

After the rabbit has been thoroughly cleaned and washed, put it into boiling water, and let it boil ten minutes; drain it, and when cold, cut it into joints, dip into beaten egg, and then in fine bread crumbs; season with salt and pepper. When all are ready fry them in butter and sweet lard, mix over a moderate fire until brown on both sides. Take them out, thicken the gravy with a spoonful of flour, turn in a cup of milk or cream; let all boil up, and turn over rabbits. Serve hot with onion sauce. (See Sauces.) Garnish with sliced lemon.

BOILED CHICKEN.

Clean, wash and stuff as for roasting. Baste a floured cloth around each and put into a pot with enough boiling water to cover them well. The hot water cooks the skin at once and prevents the escape of the juice. The broth will not be so rich as if the fowls are put on in cold water, but this proves that the meat will be more nutritious and better flavored. Stew very slowly, for the first half hour especially. Boil an hour or more, guiding yourself by size and toughness. Serve with egg, bread or oyster sauce. (See Sauces.)

CHICKEN PIE.

Prepare the chicken as for fricassee. When the chicken is stewed tender, seasoned, and the gravy thickened, take it from the fire; take out the largest bones, scrape the meat from the neck and backbone, throw the bones away; line the sides of a four or six quart pudding-dish with a rich baking powder or soda biscuit dough, a quarter of an inch thick; put in part of the chicken, a few lumps of butter, pepper and salt, if needed, some cold boiled eggs cut in slices. Add the rest of the chicken and season as before, a few new potatoes in their season might be added. Pour over the gravy, being sure to have enough to fill the dish, and cover with a crust a quarter of an inch thick, made with a hole in the center the size of a teacup.

Brush over the top with beaten white of egg and bake for half to three-quarters of an hour. Garnish the top with small bright celery leaves, neatly arranged in a circle.

FRIED CHICKEN.

Wash and cut up a young chicken, wipe it dry, season with salt and pepper, dredge it with flour, or dip each piece in beaten egg and then in cracker crumbs. Have in a frying pan one ounce each of butter and sweet lard made boiling hot. Lay in the chicken and fry brown on both sides. Take up, drain it and set aside in a covered dish. Stir into the gravy left, if not too much, a large tablespoonful of flour, make it smooth, add a cup of cream or milk, season with salt and pepper, boil up and pour over the chicken. Some like chopped parsley added to the gravy. Serve hot.

If the chicken is old, put into a stewpan with a little water and simmer gently till tender; season with salt and pepper, dip in flour or cracker crumbs and egg, and fry as above. Use the broth the chicken was cooked in to make the gravy, instead of the cream or milk, or use an equal quantity of both.

CHICKEN CROQUETTES.

Put a cup of cream or milk in a saucepan, set it over the fire, and when it boils add a lump of butter as large as an egg, in which has been mixed a tablespoonful of flour. Let it boil up thick; remove from the fire, and when cool mix into it a teaspoonful of salt, half a teaspoonful of pepper, a bit of minced onion or parsley, one cup of fine bread crumbs, and a pint of finely-chopped cooked chicken, either roasted or boiled. Lastly, beat up two eggs and work in with the whole. Flour your hands and make into small, round, flat cakes; dip in egg and bread crumbs and fry like fish cakes in butter and good sweet lard mixed, or like fried cakes in plenty of hot lard. Take them up with a skimmer and lay them on brown paper to free them from the grease. Serve hot.

ROAST DUCK. (Tame)

Pick, draw, clean thoroughly, and wipe dry. Cut the neck close to the back, beat the breast-bone flat with a rolling pin, tie the wings and legs securely, and stuff with the following:—

Three pints bread crumbs, six ounces butter, or part butter and salt pork, two chopped onions and one teaspoonful each of sage, black pepper and salt. Do not stuff very full, and sew up the openings firmly to keep the flavor in and the fat out. If not fat enough, it should be larded with salt pork, or tie a slice upon the breast. Place in a baking pan, with a little water, and baste frequently with salt and water—some add onion, and some vinegar; turn often, so that the sides and back may all be nicely browned. When nearly done, baste with butter and a little flour. These directions will apply to tame geese as well as ducks. Young ducks should roast from twenty-five to thirty minutes, and full-grown ones for an hour or more, with frequent basting. Some prefer them underdone and served very hot; but, as a rule, thorough cooking will prove more palatable. Make a gravy out of the necks and gizzards by putting them in a quart of cold water, that must be reduced to a pint by boiling. The giblets, when done, may be chopped fine and added to the juice. The preferred seasonings are one tablespoonful of Madeira or sherry, a blade of mace, one small onion, and a little cayenne pepper; strain through a hair sieve; pour a little over the ducks and serve the remainder in a boat. Serve with jellies or any tart sauce.

CHICKEN LUNCH FOR TRAVELING.

Cut a young chicken down the back; wash and wipe dry; season with salt and pepper; put in a dripping-pan and bake in a moderate oven three-quarters of an hour. This is much better for traveling lunch than when seasoned with butter.

All kinds of poultry and meat can be cooked quicker by adding to the water in which they are boiled a little vinegar or a piece of lemon. By the use of a little acid there will be a considerable saving of fuel. as well as shortening of time, Its action is beneficial on old tough meats, rendering them quite tender and easy of digestion. Tainted meats and fowls will lose their bad taste and odor if cooked in this way, and if not used too freely no taste of it will be acquired.

CHICKEN POT-PIE.

This style of pot pie was formerly used by cooks who did not consider the long cooking of the crust destructive to its spongy lightness or render it hard and dry.

Take a pair of fine fowls, cut them up, wash the pieces, and season with pepper only. Make a light biscuit dough and plenty of it, as it is always much liked by the eaters of pot pie. Roll out the dough not very thin, and cut most of it into long squares. Butter the sides of a pot, and line them with dough nearly to the top. Lay slices of cold ham at the bottom of the pot, and then the pieces of fowl, interspersed all through with squares of dough and potatoes, pared and quartered. Pour in a quart of water. Cover the whole with a lid of dough having a slit in the center, through which the gravy will bubble up. Boil it steadily for two hours. Half an hour before you take it up, put in through the hole in the centre of the crust some bits of butter rolled in flour, to thicken the gravy. When done, put the pie on a large dish, and pour the gravy over it.

You may intersperse it all through with cold ham.

A pot-pie may be made of ducks, rabbits, squirrels or venison. Also of beefsteak. A beefsteak, or some porksteaks (the lean only), greatly improve a chicken pot-pie. If you use no ham, season with salt.

BROILED PIGEONS OR SQUABS.

Split them down the back and broil the same as chicken; seasoning well with salt, pepper and plenty of butter. Broil slices of salt pork, very thin; place a slice over each bird and serve.

TO ROAST
PARTRIDGES, PHEASANTS, QUAIL OR GROUSE.

Carefully cut out all the shot, wash thoroughly but quickly, using soda in the wa' , rinse again, and dry with a clean cloth. Stuff them and sew them up. Skewer the legs and wings to the body, larder the breast with very thin slices of fat salt pork, place them in the oven, and baste with butter and water before taking up, having seasoned them with salt and pepper; or you can leave out the pork and use only butter, or cook them without stuffing. Make a gravy of the drippings thickened with browned flour. Boil up and serve in a boat.

These are all very fine broiled, first splitting down the back, placing on the gridiron the inside down, cover with a baking tin, and broil slowly at first. Serve with cream gravy.

Household Hints.

WATER.

All beings need drink as much as they need food, and it is just as necessary to health as pure air; therefore the water should be boiled or filtered before being drank. Rain-water filtered is probably the best attainable. Boiling the water destroys the vegetable and animal matter, and leaves the mineral matter deposited on the bottom of the vessel containing it; therefore it leaves it clear from poisonous substances.

HOW TO MAKE USE OF HOT WATER.

One of the simplest and most effectual means of relieving pain is by the use of hot water, externally and internally, the temperature varying according to the feelings of the patient. For bruises, sprains, and similar accidental hurts, it should be applied immediately, as hot as can be borne, by means of a cloth dipped in the water and laid on the wounded part, or by immersion, if convenient, and the treatment kept up until relief is obtained. If applied at once, the use of hot water will generally prevent, nearly, if not entirely, the bruised flesh from turning black. For pains resulting from indigestion, and known as wind colic, etc., a cupful of hot water, taken in sips, will often relieve at once. When that is insufficient, a flannel folded in several thicknesses, large enough to fully cover the painful place, should be wrung out of hot water and laid over the seat of the pain. It should be as hot as the skin can bear without injury, and be renewed every ten minutes or oftener, if it feels cool, until the pain is gone. The remedy is simple, efficient, harmless, and within the reach of every one ; and should be more generally used than it is. If used along with common sense, it might save many a doctor's bill, and many a course of drug treatment as well.

A GOOD COUGH REMEDY

Syrup of squills four ounces, syrup of tolu four ounces, tincture of bloodroot one and one-half ounces, camphorated tincture of opium four ounces. Mix. Dose for an adult, one teaspoonful repeated every two to four hours, or as often as necessary.

CURE FOR TOOTHACHE.

The worst toothacke, or neuralgia, coming from the teeth may be speedily and delightfully ended by the application of a bit of clean cotton saturated in a solution of ammonia to the defective tooth. Sometimes the late sufferer is prompted to momentary laughter by the application, but the pain will disappear.

Alum reduced to a powder, a teaspoonful of the powder and an equal quantity of fine salt well mixed, applied to the gums by dipping your moistened finger in the mixed powder ; put some also in the tooth, and keep rubbing the gums with it ; it scarcely ever fails to cure.

FOR EARACHE.

Take a bit of cotton batting, put on it a pinch of black pepper, gather it up and tie it, dip it in sweet oil, and insert it in the ear ; put a flannel bandage over the head to keep it warm ; it often gives immediate relief.

Tobacco smoke, puffed into the ear, has oftentimes been effectual.

Another remedy : Take equal parts of tincture of opium and glycerine. Mix, and from a warm teaspoon drop two or three drops into the ear, stop the ear tight with cotton, and repeat every hour or two. If matter should form in the ear, make a suds with castile soap and warm water, about 100° F., or a little more than milk warm, and have some person inject it into the ear while you hold that side of the head the lowest. If it does not heal in due time, inject a little carbolic acid and water in the proportion of one drachm of the acid to one pint of warm water each time after using the suds.

REMEDY FOR BURNS AND SCALDS.

A piece of cottonwadding, spread with butter or sweet oil, and bound on the burn instantly, will draw out the pain without leaving a scar ; also a handful of flour, bound on instantly, will prevent blistering. The object is to entirely exclude the air from the part affected. Some use common baking-soda, dry or wet, often giving instant relief, withdrawing the heat and pain. Another valuable remedy is to beat the yellow of and egg into linseed oil, and apply it with a feather on the injured part frequently. It will afford ready relief and heals with great rapidity. Some recommend the white part of the egg, which is very cooling and soothing, and soon allays the smarting pain. It is the exposure of the part coming in contact with the air that gives the extreme discomfort experienced from ordinary afflictions of this kind, and anything which excludes air and prevents inflammation is the thing to be at once applied.

CONSTIPATION.

One or two figs eaten fasting is sufficient for some, an they are especially good in the case of children, as there in no trouble in getting them to take them. A spoonful of wheaten bran in a glass of water is a simple remedy, and quite effective, taken half an hour before breakfast ; fruit eaten raw ; partake largely of laxative food ; exercise in the open air ; drink freely of cold water during the day, etc. It is impossible to give many of the numerons treatments in so short a space, suffice it to say that the general character of our diet and experience is such as to assure us that at least one-quarter of the food that we swallow is intended by nature to be evacuated from the system ; and if it is not, it is again absorbed into the system, poisoning the blood and producing much suffering and permanent disease. The evacuation of the bowels *daily*, and above all, *regularly* is therefore all important to aid this form of discrder.

COUGHS AND COLDS.

Borax has proved a most effective remedy in certain forms of colds. In sudden hoarseness or loss of voice in public speakers or singers, from colds, relief for an hour or so may be obtained by slowly dissolving, and partially swallowing, a lump of borax the size of a garden pea, or about three or four grains held in the mouth for ten or fifteen minutes before speaking or singing. This produces a profuse secretion of saliva or "watering" of the mouth and the throat, just as wetting brings back the missing notes to a flute when it is too dry.

A flannel dipped in boiling water and sprinkled with turpentine, laid on chest as quickly as possible, will relieve the most severe cold or hoarseness.

Another simple, pleasant remedy is furnished by beating up the white of one egg, adding to it the juice of one lemon, and sweetening with white sugar to taste. Take a teaspoonful from time to time. It has been known to effectually cure the ailment.

Or bake a lemon or sour orange twenty minutes in a moderate oven. When done, open at one end and take out the inside. Sweeten with sugar or molasses. This is an excellent remedy for hoarseness.

A GOOD CROUP REMEDY.

Croup, it is said, can be cured in one minute, and the remedy is simply alum and sugar. Take a knife or grater and shave off in small particles about a teaspoonful of alum ; then mix it with twice its amount of sugar, to make it palatable, and administer it as quickly as possible. Almost instantaneous relief will follow. Turpentine is said to be an excellent remedy for croup. Saturate a piece of flannel and apply it to the chest and throat, and take inwardly three or four drops on a lump of sugar.

HOW TO STOP THE FLOW OF BLOOD.

For a slight cut there is nothing better to control the hemorrhage than common unglazed brow wrapping paper, such as is used by marketmen and grocers ; a piece to be bound over the wound. A handful of flour bound on the cut. Cobwebs and brown sugar, pressed on like lint. When the blood ceases to flow, apply arnica or laudanum.

When an artery is cut the red blood spurts out at each pulsation. Press the thumb firmly over the artery near the wound, and on the side towards the heart. Press hard enough to stop the bleeding, and wait till a physician comes. The wounded person is often able to do this himself, if he has the requisite knowledge.

SORE THROAT.

Everybody has a cure for this trouble, but simple remedies appear to be most effectual. Salt and water is used by many as a gargle, but a little alum and honey dissolved in sage tea is better. An application of cloths wrung out of hot water and applied to neck, changing as often as they begin to cool, has the most potency for removing inflammation of anything we have ever tried. It should be kept up for a number of hours ; during the evening is usually the most convenient time for applying this remedy.

Cut slices of salt pork or fat bacon, simmer a few moments in hot vinegar, and apply to throat as hot as possible. When this is taken off, as the throat is relieved, put around a bandage of soft flannel. A gargle of equal parts of borax and alum, dissolved in water, is also excellent. To be used frequently.

Camphorated oil is an excellent lotion for sore throat, sore chest, aching limbs, etc. For a gargle for sore throat, put a pinch of chlorate of potash in a glass of water. Gargle the throat with it twice a day or oftener, if necessary.

DIARRHŒA.

Take tincture of Jamaica ginger one ounce, tincture of rhubarb one ounce, tincture of opium half ounce, tincture of cardamom one and one- half ounces, tincture of kino one ounce. Mix. Dose for an adult, half to one teaspoonful, repeated every two to four hours ; and for children one year old, five drops ; two years old, five to ten drops ; three years old, ten to twelve drops, and older children in proportion to age.

TO STOP NOSE BLEEDING.

Roll up a piece of paper and press it under the upper lip. In obstinate cases, blow a little gum arabic up the nostril through a quill, which will immediately stop the discharge ; powdered alum, dissolved in water, is also good. Pressure by the finger over the small artery near the ala (wing) of the nose, on the side where the blood is flowing, is said to arrest the hemorrhage immediately. Sometimes by wringing a cloth out of very hot water and laying it on the back of the neck, gives relief. Napkins wrung out of cold water must be laid across the forehead and nose, the hands dipped in cold water, and a bottle of hot water applied to the feet.

FAINTING.

Immediately place the person fainting in a lying position, with head lower than body. In this way consciousness returns immediately, while in the erect positon it often ends in death.

SPRAINS.

The white of an egg, a tablespoonful of vinegar and a tablespoonful of spirits of turpentine. Mix in a bottle, shake thoroughly, and bathe the sprain as soon as possible after the accident. This was published in *Life Secrets*, but it is re-published by request on account of its great value. It should be remembered by everyone.

An invaluable remedy for a sprain or bruise is wormwood boiled in vinegar applied hot, with enough cloths wrapped around it to keep the sprain moist.

FOR A SPRAINED ANKLE.

For a sprained ankle, the whites of eggs and powdered alum made into a plaster is almost a specific.

TO REMOVE WARTS.

Wash with water saturated with common washing-soda, and let it dry without wiping : repeat frequently they disappear. Or pass a pin through the wart and hold one end of it over the flame of a candle or lamp until the wart fires by the heat, and it will disappear.

Another treatment of warts is to pare the hard and dry skin from their tops, and then touch them with the smallest drop of strong acetic acid, taking care that the acid does not run off the wart upon the neighboring skin ; for if it does it will occasion inflammation and much pain. If this is continued once or twice daily, with regularity, paring the surface of the wart occasionally when it gets hard and dry, the wart will be soon effectually cured.

A REMEDY
FOR REMOVING CINDERS FROM THE EYE.

In most cases a simple and effective cure may be found in one or two grains of flax-seed, which can be placed in the eye without pain or injury. As they dissolve, a glutinous substance is formed, which envelops any foreign body that may be under the lid, and the whole is easily washed out. A dozen of these seeds should constitute a part of every traveler's outfit.

Another remedy for removing objects from the eye : Take a horse-hair and double it leaving a loop. If the ocject can be seen, lay the loop over it, close the eye, and the mote will come out as the hair is withdrawn. If the irritating object cannot be seen, raise the lid of the eye as high as possible and place the loop as far as you can, close the eye and roll the ball around a few times, draw out the hair, and the substance which caused the pain will be sure to come with it. This method is practiced by axe makers and other workers in steel.

EYE LOTION

The best eye-wash for granulated lids and inflammation of the eye is composed of camphor, borax and morphine, in the following proportions : To a large wine-glass of camphor water—not spirits— add two grain of morphine and six grains of borax. Pour a few drops into the palm of the hand, and hold the eye in it, opening the lid as much as possible. Do this three or four times in twenty-four hours, and you will receive great relief from pain and smarting soreness. This recipe was received from celebrated oculist, and has never failed to relieve the most inflamed eyes.

Another remedy said to be reliable : A lump of alum as large as a cranberry boiled in a teacupful of sweet milk, and the curd used as a poultice, is excellent for inflammation of the eyes.

Another wash : A cent's worth of pure, refined white copperas dissolved in a pint of water, is also a good lotion ; but label it *poison*, as it should never go near the mouth. Bathe the eyes with the mixture, either with the hands or a small piece of linen cloth, allowing some of the liquid to get under the lids.

SUNSTROKE

Wrap a wet cloth bandage over the head ; wet another cloth, folded small, square, cover it thickly with salt, and bind it on the back of the neck ; apply dry salt behind the ears. Put mustard plasters to the calves of the legs and soles of the feet. This is an effectual remedy.

COUGH SYRUP.

Take half a pound of dry hoarhound herbs, one pod of red pepper, four tablespoonfuls of ginger, boil all in three quarts of water, then strain, and add one teaspoonful of good, fresh tar and a pound of sugar. Boil slowly and stir often, until it is reduced to one quart of syrup. When cool, bottle for use. Take one or two teaspoonfuls four or six times a day.

MEDICINAL FOOD.

Spinach has a direct effect upon complaints of the kidneys; the common dandelion, used as greens, is excellent for the same trouble; asparagus purifies the blood; celery acts admirably upon the nervous system, and is a cure for rheumatism and neuralgia; tomatoes act upon the liver; beets and turnips are excellent appetizers; lettuce and cucumbers are cooling in their effects upon the system; beans are a very nutritious and strengthening vegetable; while onions, garlic, leeks chives and shallots, all of which are similar, possess medicinal virtues of a marked character, stimulating the circulatory system, and the consequent increase of the saliva and the gastric juice promoting digestion.   Red onions are an excellent diuretic, and the white ones are recommended raw as a remedy for insomnia. They are tonic, nutritious.   A soup made from onions is regarded by the French as an excellent restorative in debility of the digestive organs.   We might go through the entire list and find each vegetable possessing its especial mission of cure, and it will be plain to every housekeeper that a vegetable diet should be partly adopted, and will prove of great advantage to the health of the family.

Miscellaneous Recipes.

THE GOOD QUALITIES OF AMMONIA.

All housekeepers should keep a bottle of ammonia, as it is the most powerful and useful agent for cleaning silks, stuffs and hats, in fact cleans everything it touches. A few drops of ammonia in water will take off grease from dishes, pans, etc., and does not injure the hands as much as the use of soda and strong chemical soaps. A spoonful in a quart of warm water for cleaning paint makes it look like new, and so with everything that needs cleaning.

Spots on towels and hosiery will disappear with little trouble if a little ammonia is put into enough water to soak the articles, and they are left in it an hour or two before washing; and if a cupful is put into the water in which clothes are soaked the night before washing, the ease with which the articles can be washed, and their great whiteness and clearness when dried, will be very gratifying. Remembering the small sum paid for three quarts of ammonia of common strength, one can easily see that no bleaching preparation can be more cheaply obtained.

No articles in kitchen use are so likely to be neglected and abused as the dish-cloths and dish towels; and in washing these, ammonia, if properly used, is a greater comfort than anywhere else. Put a teaspoonful into the water in which these clothes are, or should be, washed everyday; rub soap on the towels. Put them in the water; let them stand half an hour or so; then rub them out thoroughly, rinse faithfully, and dry outdoors in clear air and sun, dish-cloths and towels need never look gray and dingy—a perpetual discomfort to all housekeepers.

A dark carpet often looks dusty soon after it has been swept, and you know it does not need sweeping again; so wet a cloth or a sponge, wring it almost dry, and wipe off the dust. A few drops of ammonia in the water will brighten the colors.

For cleaning hair-brushes it is excellent; put a tablespoonful into the water, having it only tepid, and dip up and down until clean; then dry with the brushes down and they will be like new ones.

When employed in washing anything that is not especially soiled, use the waste water afterward for the house plants that are taken down from their usual position and immersed in the tub of water. Ammonia is a fertilizer, and helps to keep healthy the plants it nourishes. In every way, in fact, ammonia is the housekeeper's friend.

Ammonia is not only useful for cleaning, but as a household medicine. Half a teaspoonful taken in half a tumbler of water is far better for faintness than alcoholic stimulants. In the Temperance Hospital, in London, it is used with the best results. It was used freely by Lieutenant Greely's Arctic party for keeping up circulation. It is a relief in nervousness, headache and heart disturbances.

HOW TO DESTROY INSECTS AND VERMIN.

Dissolve two pounds of alumn in three or four quarts of water. Let it remain over night till all the alum is dissolved. Then with a brush, apply boiling hot to every joint or crevice in the closet or shelves where croton bugs, ants, cockroaches, etc., intrude; also to the joints and crevices of bedsteads, as bed bugs dislike it as much as croton bugs, roaches, or ants. Brush all the cracks in the floor and mopboards. Keep it boiling hot while using.

To keep woolens and furs from moths, be sure that none are in the articles when they are put away; then take a piece of strong brown paper, with not a hole through which a pin can enter. Put the article in it with several lumps of gum camphor between the folds; place this in a close box or trunk. Cover every joint with paper. A piece of cotton cloth, if thick and firm, will answer. Wherever a knitting-needle can pass, the parent moth can enter.

Place pieces of camphor, cedar-wood, Russia leather, tobacco-leaves, whole cloves, or anything strongly aromatic, in the drawers or boxes where furs and other things to be preserved from moths are kept and they will never be harmed. Mice never get into drawers or trunks where gum camphor is placed.

Another Recipe—Mix half a pint of alcohol, the same quantity of turpentine and two ounces of camphor. Keep in a stone bottle and shake well before using. The clothes or furs are to be wrapped in linen, and crumbled-up pieces of blotting-paper dipped in the liquid to be placed in the box with them, so that it smells strong. This requires renewing but once a year.

Another authority says that a positive, sure recipe is this: Mix equal quantities of pulverized borax, camphor gum and saltpetre together making a powder. Sprinkle it dry under the edges of carpets, in drawers, trunks, etc.,etc. It will also keep out all kinds of insects if plentifully used. If the housekeeper will begin at the top of her house with a powder bellows and a large quantity of this fresh powder, and puff it thoroughly into every crack and crevice, whether or not there are croton bugs in them, to the very bottom of her house special attention being paid to old furniture, closets, and wherever croton water is introduced, she will be freed from these torments. The operation may require a repetition, but the end is success.

MOTHS.

If you fear that they are at work at the edge cf the carpet, it will sometimes suffice to lay a wet towel, and press a hot flat-iron over it; but the best way is to take the carpet up, and clean it, and give a good deal of attention to the floor. Look in the cracks, and if you discover signs of moths, wash the floor with benzine, and scatter red pepper on it before putting the carpet lining down.

Heavy carpets sometimes do not require taking up every year, unless in constant use. Take out the tacks from these, fold the carpets back wash the floor in strong suds with a tablespoonful of borax dissolved in it. Dash with insect powder, or lay with tobacco leaves along the edge, and re-tack. Or use turpentine, the enemy of buffalo moths, carpet worms and other insects that injure and destroy carpets. Mix the turpentine with pure water in the proportion of three tablespoonfuls to three quarts of water, and then after the carpet has been well swept, go over each breadth carefully with a sponge dipped in the solution and wrung nearly dry. Change the water as often as it becomes dirty. The carpet will be nicely cleaned as well as disinfected. All moths can be kept away and the eggs destroyed, by this means. Spots may be renovated by the use of ox-gall or ammonia and water.

A good way to brighten a carpet is to put a half tumbler of spirits of turpentine in a basin of water, and dip your broom in it sweep over the carpet once or twice and it will restore the color and brighten it up until you would think it new. Another good way to clean old carpets is to rub them over with meal; just dampen it a very little and rub the carpet with it and when perfectly dry, sweep over with meal. After a carpet is thoroughly swept, rub it with a cloth dipped in water and ammonia; it will brighten the colors and make it look like new.

HOW TO REMOVE GREASE SPOTS.

Cold water, a tablespoonful of ammonia and soap, will take out machine grease where other means would not answer on account of colors running, etc.

TO PREVENT FLANNELS FROM SHRINKING WHEN WASHED.

The first thing to consider in washing flannels so that they retain their size, is that the article to be *washed* and *rinsed* in water the *same temperature*, that is about as warm as the hands can bear and and not allowed to cool between. The water should be a strong suds. Rub through two soapy waters; wring them out, and put into plenty of clear, clean, warm water to rinse. Then into another of the same temperature, blued a little. Wring, shake them well and hang up. Do not take out this warm water and hang out in a freezing air, as that certainly tends to shrink them. It is better to dry them in the house unless the sun shines. They should dry *quickly*. Colored flannels should never be washed in the same water after white clothes, or they will be covered, when dry, with lint; better be washed in a water by themselves. In washing worsted, such as merino dress goods, pursue the same course, only do not wring them hard; shake, hang them up and let drain. While a little damp, bring in and press smoothly on the wrong side with as hot an iron as can be used without scorching the goods.

Flannels that have become yellow from being badly washed, may be nicely whitened by soaking them two or three hours in a lather made of one-quarter of a pound of soft soap, two tablespoonfuls of powdered borax and two tablespoonfuls of carbonate of ammonia, dissolved in five or six gallons of water.

HOW TO LAUNDRY SHIRTS

To three tablespoonfuls of dry, fine starch allow a quart of water. First wet the starch smooth in a little cold water in a tin pan, put into it a little pinch of salt and a piece of enamel, or shirt polish the size of a bean, or a piece of clean tallow, or a piece of butter the size of a cranberry; pour over this a quart of *boiling* water, stirring rapidly, placing it over the fire. Cook until clear, then remove it from the fire and set the pan in another of warm water to keep the starch warm.

Turn the shirt wrong side out and dip the bosom in the hot starch as warm as the hands can bear the heat; rub the starch evenly through linen, saturating it thoroughly, wring hard to make dry as possible. Starch the collar and wristbands the same way, then hang them out to dry. Three hours before ironing them, wet the bosoms and cuffs in cold water, wring out, shake and fold, roll up tightly, wrap in a towel and let remain two or three hours.

The back of the shirt should be ironed first by doubling it lengthwise through the centre, the wristbands may be ironed next, and both sides of the sleeves, then the colar band; now place a bosom board under the bosom and with a fresh clean napkin dampened a little, rub the bosom from top towards the bottom, arranging and smoothing each plait neatly; then with a smooth, moderately - hot flat-iron, begin ironing from the top downward, pressing hard until the bosom becomes smooth, dry and glossy. Remove the bosom board and iron the front, fold both sides of the shirt towards the centre of the back, fold together below the bosom and hang on the bars to air.

TO CLEAN BLACK LACE.

A teaspoonful of gum arabic dissolved in one teacupful of boiling water; when cool, add half a teaspoonful of black ink; dip the lace and spread smoothly between the folds of a newspaper and press dry with books or the like. Lace shawls can be dressed over in this way, by pinning a sheet to the carpet and stretching the shawl upon that; or black lace can be cleaned the same as ribbon and silk. Take an old kid glove (black preferable), no matter how old, and boil it in a pint of water for a short time; then let it cool until the leather can be taken in the hand without burning; use the glove to sponge off the ribbon; if the ribbon it very dirty, dip it into water and draw through the fingers a few times before sponging. After cleaning, lay a piece of paper over the ribbon and iron; paper is etter than cloth. The ribbon will look like new.

TO CLEAN SILKS AND RIBBONS.

Half a pint of gin, half a pound of honey, half a pound of soft soap, one-eighth of a pint of water.

Mix the above ingredients together; then lay each breadth of silk upon a clean kitchen table or dresser, and scrub it well on the soiled side with the mixture. Have ready three vessels of cold water; take each piece of silk at two corners, and dip it up and down in each vessel, but do not wring it; and take care that each breadth has one vessel of quite clean water for the last dip. Hang it up dripping for a minute or two, then dab in a cloth, and iron it quickly with a very hot iron.

TO WASH WHITE LACE.

First, the soiled laces should be carefully removed from the garment and folded a number of times, keeping the edges evenly together, then basted with a coarse thread without a knot in the end. Now put them in a basin of luke-warm suds. After soaking a half hour, rub them carefully between the hands, renewing the suds several times; then, after soaping them well, place them in *cold* water and let them come to a scald. Take them from this and rinse them thoroughly in luke-warm water, blued a very little, then dip them into a *very thin*, clear starch, allowing a teaspoonful of starch to a pint of water, so thin that it will be scarcely perceptible. Now roll them in a clean, fresh towel without taking out the bastings; let them lie for an hour or more; iron over several thicknesses of flannel, taking out the bastings of one piece at a time, and ironing on the wrong side, with a moderately-hot iron; the laces should be nearly dry, and the edges and points pulled gently with the fingers into shape, before ironing.

TO CLEAN BLACK DRESS SILKS.

One of the things "not generally known," at least in this country is the Parisian method of cleaning black silk; the *modus operandi* is very simple, and the result infinitely superior to that achieved in any other manner. The silk must be thoroughly brushed and wiped with a cloth, then laid flat on a board or table, and well sponged with hot coffee, thoroughly freed from sediment by being strained through muslin. The silk is sponged on the side intended to show; it is allowed to become partially dry, and then ironed on the wrong side. The coffee removes every particle of grease, and restores the brilliancy of silk, without imparting to it either the shiny appearance or crackly and papery stiffness obtained by beer, or indeed, any other liquid. The silk really appears thickened by the process and this good effect is permanent. Our readers who will experimentalize on an apron or cravat, will never again try any other method.

HOW TO WASH AND CURL FEATHERS.

Wash in warm soap-suds and rinse in water a very little blued; if the feather is white, then let the wind dry it. When the curl has come out by washing the feather or getting it damp, place a hot flat-iron so that you can hold the feather just above it while curling. Take a bone or silver knife, and draw the fibres of the feathers between the thumb and the dull edge of the knife, taking not more than three fibres at a time, beginning at the point of the feather and curling one-half the other way. The hot iron makes the curl more durable. After a little practice one can make them look as well as new feathers. Or they can be curled by holding them over the stove or range, not near enough to burn; withdraw and shake out; then hold them over again, until they curl. When swansdown becomes soiled, it can be washed and look as good as new. Tack strips on a piece of muslin and wash in warm water with white soap then rinse and hang in the wind to dry. Rip from the muslin and rub carefully between the fingers to soften the leather.

HOW TO FRESHEN FURS.

Furs when taken out in the fall are often found to have a mussed crushed-out appearance. They can be made to look like new, by following these simple directions: Wet the fur with a hair-brush, brushing up the wrong way of the fur. Leave it to dry in the air for about half an hour, and then give it a good beating on the right side with a rattan. After beating it, comb it with a coarse comb, combing up the right way of the fur.

DRESS MENDING.

A novel way of mending a woolen or silk dress in which a round hole has been torn, and where only a patch could remedy matters, is the following: The frayed portions around the tear should be carefully smoothed, and a piece of the material, moistened with very thin mucilage, placed under the hole. A heavy weight should be put upon it until it is dry, when it is only possible to discover the mended place by careful observation.

TO GIVE CLOTHES A POLISHED FINISH IN IRONING.

Take one ounce of spermaceti and one ounce of white wax; melt and run it into a thin cake on a plate. A piece the size of a quarter dollar added to a quart of prepared starch gives a beautiful lustre to the clothes and prevents the iron from sticking.

FOR CLEANING JEWELRY.

For cleaning jewelry there is nothing better than ammonia and water. If very dull or dirty, rub a little soap on a soft brush and brush them in this wash, rinse in cold water, dry first in an old handkerchief and then rub with buck or chamois skin. Their freshness and brilliancy when thus cleaned cannot be surpassed by any compound used by jewelers.

TO CLEAN SILVER WARE.

Wash well in strong, warm soap-suds, rinse and wipe dry with a dry, soft cloth; then mix as much hartshorn powder as will be required into a thick paste, with cold water; spread this over the silver, with a soft cloth, and leave it for a little time to dry. When perfectly dry, brush it off with a clean soft cloth, or brush and polish it with a piece of chamois skin. Hartshorn is one of the best possible ingredients for plate powder for daily use. It leaves on the silver a deep, dark polish, and at the same time does not injure it. Whiting, dampened with liquid ammonia, is excellent also.

TO WASH COLORED GARMENTS.

Delicately colored socks and stockings are apt to fade in washing. If they are soaked for a night in a pail of tepid water containing a half pint of turpentine, then wrung out and dried, the colors will 'set,'' and they can afterwards be washed without fading.

For calicoes that fade, put a teaspoonful of sugar of lead into a pailful of water and soak the garment fifteen minutes before washing.

TO REMOVE STAINS FROM MARBLE.

Mix together one-half pound of soda, one-half pound of soft soap and one pound of whiting. Boil them until they become as thick as paste, and let it cool. Before it is quite cold, spread it over the surface of the marble and leave it at least a whole day. Use soft water to wash it off, and rub it well with soft cloths. For a black marble, nothing is better than spirits of turpentine.

Another paste answers the same purpose: Take two parts of soda, one of pumice stone and one of finely-powdered chalk. Sift these through a fine sieve and mix them into a paste with water. Rub this well all over the marble and the stains will be removed; then wash it with soap and water and a beautiful bright polish will be produced.

TO REMOVE STAINS AND SPOTS.

Children's clothes, table linens, towels, etc., should be thoroughly examined before wetting, as soap-suds, washing-fluids, etc., will fix almost any stain past removal. Many stains will pass away by being simply washed in pure, soft water; or alcohol will remove, before the article has been in soap-suds, many stains; iron mold, mildew, or almost any similar spot, can be taken out by dipping in diluted citric acid; then cover with salt and lay in the bright sun till the stain disappears. If of long standing, it may be necessary to repeat the wetting and the sunlight. Be careful to rinse in several waters as soon as the stain is no longer visible. Ink, fruit, wine, and mildew stains must first be washed in clear, cold water, removing as much of the spots as can be; then mix one teaspoonful of oxalic acid and a half pint of rain-water. Dip the stain in this and wipe off in clear water. Wash at once, if a fabric that will bear washing. A tablespoonful of white currant juice, if any can be had, is even better than lemon. This preparation may be used on the most delicate articles without injury. Shake it up before using it. Mark it "poison," and put it where it will not be meddled with.

TO REMOVE OIL STAINS.

Benzine is most effectual, not only for silk but for any other material whatever. It can be procured from any druggist. By simply covering both sides of greased silk with magnesia, and allowing it to remain for a few hours, the oil is absorbed by the powder. Should the first application be insufficient, it may be repeated, and even rubbed in with the hand. Should the silk be Tussah or Indian silk, it will wash.

To remove an acid stain on violet silk: Brush the discoloration with tincture of iodine, then saturate the spot well with a solution of hypo sulphite of soda, and dry gradually. This restores the original color perfectly.

Muriatic acid is successfully used for removing ink stains and iron mold on a number of colors which it does not attack.

Sulphurous acid is only employed for whitening undyed goods, straw hats, etc., and for removing the stains of certain fruits on silks and woolens. Sulphurous gas is also used for this purpose, but the liquid gas is safer.

Oxalic acid is used for removing ink and rust stains, and remnants of mud stains, which do not yield to other deterrents. It may also be used for destroying the stains of fruits and astringent juices, and old stains of urine. However, its use is limited to white goods, as it attacks fugitive colors, and even light shades of those reputed to be fast. The best method of applying it is to dissolve it in cold or luke-warm water, to let it remain a moment upon the spot, and then rub it with the fingers. Wash out in clear, warm water immediately.

Citric acid serves to revive and brighten certain colors, especially greens and yellows. It restore scarlets which have been turned to a crimson by the action of alkalies. Acetic acid or tartaric acid may be used instead.

Where it is feared that soap may change the color of an article, as, for instance, scarlet hosiery or lilac print, if the garment be not badly soiled, it may be cleansed by washing without soap in water in which pared potatoes have been boiled. This method will also prevent color from running in washing prints.

To prevent blue from running into a white ground, dissolve a teaspoonful of copperas in a pailful of soft water, add a piece of lime the size of an acorn, and soak the garments in this water two hours before washing. To keep colors from running in washing black prints, put a teaspoonful of black pepper in the first water.

Salt or beef's gall in the water helps to set black. A tablespoonful of spirits of turpentine to a gallon of water sets most blues, and alum is very efficacious in setting green. Black or very dark calicoes should be stiffened with gum arabic—five cents' worth is enough for a dress. If however, starch is used, the garment should be turned wrong side out.

A simple way to remove grass stains is to spread butter on them, and lay the article in hot sunshine, or wash in alcohol. Fruit stains upon cloth or the hands may be removed by rubbing with the juice of ripe tomatoes. If applied immediately, powdered starch will also take fruit stains out of table linen. Left on the spot for a few hours, it absorbs every trace of the stain.

For mildew stains or iron rust, mix together soft soap, laundry starch, half as much salt, and the juice of a lemon. Apply to the spots and spread the garment on the grass. Or wet the linen, rub into it white soap, then finely powdered chalk; lay upon the grass and keep damp. Old mildew stains may be removed by rubbing yellow soap on both sides and afterwards laying on, very thick, starch which has been dampened. Rub in well and expose to light and air.

There are several effectual methods of removing grease from cloths. First, wet with a linen cloth dipped in chloroform. Second mix four tablespoonfuls of alcohol with one tablespoonful of salt; shake together until the salt is dissolved and apply with a sponge. Third, wet with weak ammonia water; then lay a thin white blotting or tissue paper over it, and iron lightly with an iron not too hot. Fourth, apply a mixture of equal parts of alcohol, gin and ammonia. Candle grease yields to a warm iron. Place a piece of blotting or other absorbing paper under the absorbing fabric; put a piece of the paper also on the spot, apply warm iron to the paper and as soon as a spot of grease appears, move the paper and press again until the spot disappears. Lard will remove wagon grease. Rub the spot with the lard as if washing it, and when it is well out, wash in the ordinary way with soap and water until thoroughly cleansed.

To make linen beautifully white, prepare the water for washing by putting into every ten gallons a large handful of powdered borax or boil with the clothes one teaspoonful of spirits of turpentine.

Fruit stains may be taken out by boiling water. Place the material over a basin or other vessel and pour the boiling water from the kettle over the stain.

Pure water, cold or hot, mixed with acids, serves for rinsing goods in order to remove foreign and neutral bodies which cover the color. Steam softens fatty matters and thus facilitates their removal by reagents.

Sulphuric acid may be used in certain cases, particularly for brightening and raising greens, reds, yellows, etc., but it must be diluted with at least one hundred times its weight of water and more in cases of delicate shades.

TO PREVENT LAMP-WICKS FROM SMOKING.
Soak them in vinegar, and then dry them thoroughly.

TO CLEAN CARPETS.
Carpets after the dust has been beaten out may be brightened by scattering upon them corn meal mixed with salt and then sweeping it off. Mix salt and meal in equal proportions. Carpets should be thoroughly beaten on the wrong side first and then on the right side, after which spots may be removed by the use of ox-gall or ammonia and water.

REMOVING INK FROM CARPETS.

When freshly spilled, ink can be removed from carpets by wetting in milk. Take cotton batting and soak up all of the ink that it will receive, being careful not to let it spread. Then take fresh cotton, wet in milk, and sop it up carefully. Repeat this operation, changing cotton and milk each time. After most of the ink has been taken up in this way, with fresh cotton and clean, rub the spot. Continue till all disappears; then wash the spot in clean warm water and a little soap; rinse in clear water and rub till nearly dry. If the ink is dried in, we know of no way that will not take the color from the carpet as well as the ink, unless the ink is on a white spot. In that case, salts of lemon, or soft soap, starch and lemon juice, will remove the ink as easily as if on cotton.

HOW TO TAKE OUT INDELIBLE INK STAINS.

Most indelible inks contain nitrate of silver, the stain of which may be removed by first soaking in a solution of common salt, and afterward washing with ammonia. Or use solution of ten grains of cyanide of potassium and five grains of iodine to one ounce of water, or a solution of eight parts each bichloride of mercury and chloride of ammonium in one hundred and twenty-five parts of water.

TO BLEACH COTTON CLOTH.

Take one large spoonful of sal soda and one pound of chloride lime for thirty yards; dissolve in clean, soft water; rinse the cloth thoroughly in cold, soft water so that it may not rot. This amount of cloth may be bleached in fourteen or fifteen minutes.

TO SOFTEN WATER.

Add half a pound of the best quick-lime dissolved in water to every hundred gallons. Smaller proportions may be more conveniently managed, and if allowed to stand a short time the lime will have united with the carbonate of lime, and been deposited at the bottom of the receptacle. Another way is to put a gallon of lye into a barrelful of water, or two or three shovelfuls of wood-ashes, let stand over night; it will be clear and soft.

SOFT SOAP WITHOUT COOKING.

Pour two pailfuls of boiling water upon twenty pounds of potash and let it stand two hours. Have ready thirty pounds of clean grease, upon which pour one pailful of the lye, adding another pail of water to the potash; let it stand three or four hours, stir it well; then pour a gallon of the lye upon the grease, stir it well; and in half an hour another gallon of the lye, stir it thoroughly; in half an hour repeat the process, and thus proceed until you have poured off all the lye; then add two pails of boiling hot water to the remainer of the potash, and let it stand ten hours; then stir the mixture, and if it has become stiff and the grease has disappeared from the surface, take out a little and see whether the weak lye will thicken it; if it does, add the lye; if it does not, try water, and if that thickens it, let it stand another day, stirring it well five or six times during the day; if the lye does not separate from the grease you may fill up with water.

OLD-STYLE SOFT SOAP.

To *set the leach*, bore several holes in the bottom of a barrel, or use one without a bottom; prepare a board larger than the barrel, then set the barrel on it, and cut a groove around just outside the barrel, making one groove from this to the edge of the board, to carry off the lye as it runs off, with a groove around it, running into one in the centre of the board. Place all two feet from the ground and tip it so that the lye may run easily from the board into the vessel below prepared to receive it. Put half bricks or stones around the edge of the inside of the barrel; place on them one end of some sticks about two inches wide, inclining to the centre; on those place some straw to the depth of two inches, over it scatter two pounds of slaked lime. Put in ashes, about half of a bushel at a time, pack it well, by pounding it down, and continue doing so until the barrel is full, leaving a funnel-shaped hollow in the centre large enough to hold several quarts of water. Use rain-water boiling hot. Let the water disappear before adding more. If the ashes are packed very *tightly* it may require two or three days before the lye will begin to run, but it will be the stronger for it, and much better.

WASHING FLUID.

One gallon of water and four pounds of ordinary washing soda, and a quarter of a pound of soda. Heat the water to boiling hot, put in the soda, boil about five minutes, then pour it over two pounds of unslaked lime, let it bubble and foam until it settles, turn it off and bottle it for use. This is the article that is used in the Chinese laundries for whitening their linen, and is called "Javelle water;" a tablespoonful put into a suds of three gallons, and a little, say a quarter of a cupful, in the boiler when boiling the clothes, makes them very white and clear. Must be well rinsed afterwards. This preparation will remove tea stains and almost all ordinary stains of fruit, grass, etc. This fluid brightens the colors of colored clothes, does not rot them, but should not be *left long in any water;* the boiling, sudsing, rinsing and bluing, should be done in quick succession, until the clothes are ready to hang on the line.

A GOOD HARD SOAP FOR WASHING.

Six pounds of washing soda and three of unslaked lime. Pour on four gallons of boiling water, let it stand until perfectly clear, then drain off, and put in six pounds of clean fat. Boil it until it begins to to harden, about two hours, stirring most of the time. While boiling, thin it with two gallons of cold water, which you have previously poured on the alkaline mixture, after draining off the four gallons. This must be settled clear before it is drawn off. Add it when there is danger of boiling over. Try the thickness by cooling a little on a plate. Put in a handful of salt just before taking from the fire. Wet a tub to prevent sticking; turn in the soap and let it stand until solid. Cut into bars, put on a board and let it dry. This makes about forty pounds of soap. It can be flavored just as you turn it out.

BOILED SOFT SOAP.

Put in a kettle the grease consisting of all kinds of fat that has accumulated in the kitchen, such as scraps and bones from the soup-kettle, rinds from meat, etc.; fill the kettle half full; if there is too much grease it can be skimmed off after the soap is cold, for another kettle of soap. This is the only true test when enough grease is used, as the lye will consume all that is needed and no more. Make a fire under one side of it. The kettle should be in an out-house or out of doors. Let it heat very hot so as to fry; stir occasionally to prevent burning. Now put in the lye a gallon at a time, watching it closely until it boils, as it sometimes runs over at the beginning. Add lye until the kettle is full enough, but not *too full to boil well*. Soap should boil from the *side* and not the middle, as this would be more likely to cause it to boil over. To test the soap, to one spoonful of soap add one of rain-water; if it stirs up very thick, the soap is good and will keep; if it becomes thinner, it is not good. This is the result of one of three causes, either it is too weak, or there is a deposit of dirt, or it is too strong. Continue to boil for a few hours, when it should flow from the stick with which it is stirred like thick molasses; but if after boiling it remains thin, let it stand over night, removing it from the fire, then draining it off very carefully into another vessel, being very particular to prevent any sediment from passing. Wash the kettle, return the soap and boil again, if dirt was the cause; it will now be thick and good; otherwise, if it was *too strong*, rain-water added will make it right, adding the water gradually until right and just thick enough.

TO RENEW OLD CRAPE

Place a little water in a tea-kettle, and let it boil until there is plenty of steam from the spout; then, holding the crape in both hands, pass it to and fro several times through the steam, and it will be clean and look nearly equal to new.

Facts Worth Knowing.

TO CLEAN BRASS WARE.

Mix one ounce oxalic acid, six ounces of rotten stone, all in powder, one ounce of sweet oil, and sufficient water to make a paste. Apply a small portion, and rub dry with a flannel or leather. The liquid dip most generally used consists of nitric and sulphuric acids ; but this is more corrosive.

TO REMOVE ODOR
OF ONION FROM COOKING UTENSILS.

Put wood-ashes or sal soda, potash or lye ; fill with water and let it stand on the stove until it boils ; then wash in hot suds, and rinse well.

TO KEEP MILK SWEET.

Put into a panful a spoonful of grated horse radish, it will keep it sweet for days.

POISON WATER.

Water boiled in galvanized iron becomes poisonous, and cold water passed through zinc-lined iron pipes should never be used for cooking or drinking. Hot water for cooking should never be taken from hot water pipes ; keep a supply heated in kettles.

VENTILATION IN A ROOM.

Place a pitcher of cold water on a table in your room and it will absorb all the gases with which the room is filled from the respiration of those eating or sleeping in the apartment. Very few realize how important such purification is for the health of the family or indeed, understand or realize that there can be any impurity in the rooms ; yet in a few hours a pitcher or pail of cold water—the colder the more effective—will make the air of a room pure, but the water will be entirely unfit for use.

TO REMOVE SPOTS FROM WASH GOODS.

Rub them with the yolk of egg before washing.

TO TAKE OUT PAINT.

Equal parts of ammonia and turpentine will take paint out of clothing, no matter how dry or hard it may be. Saturate the spot two or three times, then wash out in soap-suds. Ten cents' worth of oxalic acid dissolved in a pint of hot water will remove paint spots from the windows. Pour a little into a cup, and apply to the spots with a swab, but be sure not to allow the acid to touch the hands. Brasses may be quickly cleaned with it. Great care must be exercised in labeling the bottle, and putting it out of the reach of children, as it is a deadly poison.

TO REMOVE TAR FROM CLOTH.

Saturate the spot and rub well with turpentine, and every trace of tar will be removed.

TO DESTROY ANTS.

Ants that frequent houses or gardens may be destroyed by taking flour of brimstone half a pound, and potash four ounces ; set them in an iron or earthen pan over the fire until dissolved and united ; afterwards beat them to a powder, and infuse a little of this powder in water, and wherever you sprinkle it the ants will fly the place.

HICCOUGH CURE.

Sit erect and inflate the lungs fully. Then retaining the breath, bend forward slowly until the chest meets the knees. After slowly rising again to the erect position, slowly exhale the breath. Repeat this process a second time, and the nerves will be found to have received an access of energy that will enable them to perform their natural functions.

TO REMOVE INK, WINE OR FRUIT STAINS.

Saturate well in tomato juice; it is also an excellent thing to remove stains from the hands.

TO REMOVE WHITE SPOTS
FROM VARNISHED FURNITURE.

Hold a hot stove lid or plate over them and they will soon disappear.

TO PREVENT ANTS.

A heavy chalk mark laid a finger's distance from your sugar box and all around (there must be no space not covered) will surely prevent ants from troubling.

TO REMOVE FINGER-MARKS ON FURNITURE.

Sweet oil will remove finger-marks from varnished furniture, and kerosene from oiled furniture.

TO REMOVE PAINT FROM BLACK SILK.

Patient rubbing with chloroform will remove paint from black silk or any other goods, and will not hurt the most delicate color or fabric.

SLICING PINEAPPLES.

The knife used for peeling a pineapple should not be used for slicing it, as the rind contains an acid that is apt to cause a swollen mouth and sore lips. The Cubans use salt as an antidote for the ill effects of the peel.

TO TOUGHEN
LAMP-CHIMNEYS AND GLASS-WARE.

Immerse the article in a pot filled with cold water, to which some common salt has been added. Boil the water well, then cool slowly. Glass treated in this way will resist any sudden change of temperature.

CHOKING.

A piece of food lodged in the throat may someti.nes be pushed down with the finger, or removed with a hair-pin quickly straightened and hooked at the end, or by two or three vigorous blows on the back between the shoulders.

TO PREVENT COCKROACHES.

Hellebore sprinkled on the floor at night. They eat it and are poisoned.

Toilet Recipes, Items.

JOCKEY CLUB BOUQUET.

Mix one pint extract of rose, one pint extract of tuberose half a pint of extract of cassia four ounces extract of jasmine, and three ounces tincture of civet.   Filter the mixture.

ROSE-WATER.

Preferable to the distilled for a perfume, or for culinary purposes. Attar of rose, twelve drops : rub it up with half an ounce of white sugar and two drachms carbonate magnesia ; then add gradually one quart of water and two ounces of proof spirit, and filter through paper.

BAY RUM.

French proof spirit one gallon, extract bay six ounces.   Mix and color with caramel ; needs no filtering.

LAVENDER WATER.

Oil of lavender two ounces, orris root holf an ounce, spirits of wine one pint.   Mix and keep two or three weeks.   It may then be strained through two thicknesses of blotting-paper and is ready for use.

COLD CREAM.

Melt one ounce oil of almonds, half ounce spermaceti, one drachm white wax, and then add two ounces of rose-water, and stir it constantly until cold.

FOR DANDRUFF.

Take glycerine four ounces, tincture of cantharides five ounces, bay rum four ounces, water two ounces.   Mix, and apply once a day and rub well down the scalp.

HAIR WASH.

One penny's worth of borax, half a pint of olive oil, one pint of boiling water. Pour the boiling water over the borax and oil; let it cool; then put the mixture into a bottle. Shake it before using, and apply it with a flannel. Camphor and borax, dissolved in boiling water and left to cool, make a very good wash for the hair; as also does rosemary water mixed with a little borax. After using any of these washes, when the hair becomes thoroughly dry, a little pomatum or oil should be rubbed in to make it smooth and glossy — that is, if one prefers oil on the hair.

TOILET OR FACE POWDER.

Take a quarter of a pound of wheat starch pounded fine; sift it through a fine sieve, or a piece of lace; add to it eight drops of oil of rose, oil of lemon thirty drops, oil of bergamot fifteen drops. Rub thoroughly together.

The French throw this powder into alcohol, shaking it, letting it settle, then pouring off the alcohol and drying the powder. In that case, the perfume is added lastly.

TO REMOVE FRECKLES.

The following lotion is highly recommended : One ounce of lemon juice, a quarter of a drachm of powdered borax, and half a drachm of sugar; mix in a bottle, and allow them to stand a few days, when the liquor should be rubbed occasionally on the hands and face. Another application is : Friar's balsam one part, rosewater twenty parts.

HAIR INVIGORATOR.

Bay rum two pints, alcohol one pint, castor oil one ounce, carb, ammonia half an ounce, tincture of cantharides one ounce. Mix them well. This compound will promote the growth of the hair and prevent it from falling out.

TO REMOVE INK STAINS FROM LINEN.

Dip the ink spot in pure melted tallow, then wash out the tallow and the ink will come out with it. This is said to be unfailing. Milk will remove ink from linen or colored muslins, when acids would be ruinous, by soaking the goods until the spot is very faint and then rubbing and rinsing in cold water.

TO REMOVE PIMPLES.

One teaspoonful of carbolic acid and one pint of rose-water mixed is an excellent remedy for pimples. Bathe the skin thoroughly and often, but do not let the wash get into the eyes.

This wash is soothing to mosquito bites, and irritations of the skin of every nature.

It is advisable, in order to clear the complexion permanently, to cleanse the blood ; then the wash would be of advantage.

To obtain a good complexion a person's diet should receive the first attention. Greasy food, highly spiced soups, hot bread and butter, meats or game, rich gravies, alcoholic liquors, coffee—all are injurious to the complexion. Strong tea used daily will after a time give the skin the color and appearance of leather. Coffee affects the nerves more, but the skin less, and a healthy nervous system is necessary to beauty. Eating between meals, late suppers, over-eating at meals eating sweetmeats, candies, etc., all these tend to disorder the blood, producing pimples and blotches.

Washing of the face or skin is another consideration for a good complexion ; it should be thoroughly washed in plenty of luke-warm water with some mild soap—then rinsed in clear water *well;* dry with a thick soft towel. If suds is left or wiped off the skin, the action of the air and sun will tan the surface, and permanently deface the complexion ; therefore one should be sure to thoroughly rinse off all soap from the skin to avoid the tanning, which will leave a brown or yellow tinge impossible to efface.

TOOTH POWDER.

Prepared chalk half a pound, powdered myrrh two ounces, camphor two drachms, orris root, powdered, two ounces; moisten the camphor with alcohol and mix well together.

REMOVING TARTAR FROM THE TEETH.

This preparation is used by dentists. Pure muriatic acid one ounce, water one ounce, honey two ounces, mix thoroughly. Take a tooth-brush, and wet it freely with this preparation, and briskly rub the black teeth, and in a moment's time they will be perfectly white; then immediately wash out the mouth well with water, that the acid may not act on the enamel of the teeth. This should be done only occasionally.

BAD BREATH.

Bad breath from catarrh, foul stomach, or bad teeth, may be temporarily relieved by diluting a little bromo chloralum with eight or ten parts of water, and using it as a gargle, and swallowing a few drops before going out. A pint of bromo chloralum costs fifty cents, but a small vial will last a long time.

SHAVING COMPOUND.

Half a pound of plain, white soap, dissolved in a small quantity of alcohol, as little as can be used; add a tablespoonful of pulverized borax. Shave the soap and put it in a small tin basin or cup; place it on the fire in a dish of boiling water; when melted, add the alcohol, and remove from the fire; stir in oil of bergamot sufficient to perfume it.

SHAMPOO MIXTURE.

Dissolve half an ounce of carbonate of ammonia and one ounce of borax in one quart of water; then add two ounces of glycerine in three quarts of New England rum, and one quart of bay rum. Moisten the hair with this liquid, shampoo with the hands until a light lather is formed; then wash off with plenty of clean water.

TO REMOVE MOTH PATCHES.

Into a pint of rum put a tablespoonful of flour of sulphur. Apply this to the patches once a day, and they will disappear in two or three weeks.

TOILET SOAP.

One pound of washing soda, one pound of lard or clear tallow, half a pound of unslacked lime, one tablespoonful of salt, three quarts of water. Put the soda and lime in a large dish, and pour over the water, boiling hot ; stir until dissolved ; let it stand until clear, then pour off the clear liquid, add the grease and salt ; boil four hours, then pour into pans to cool. If it should be inclined to curdle or separate, indicating the lime to be too strong, pour in a little more water, and boil again. Perfume as you please, and pour into molds or a shallow dish, and, when cold, cut into bars to dry.

TOILET ITEMS.

Mutton tallow is considered excellent to soften the hands. It may be rubbed on at any time when the hands are perfectly dry, but the best time is when retiring, and an old pair of soft, large gloves thoroughly covered on the inside with the tallow and glycerine in equal parts, melted together, can be worn during the night with the most satisfactory results.

Four parts of glycerine and five parts of yolks of eggs thoroughly mixed, and applied after washing the hands, is also considered excellent.

For chapped hands or face : One ounce of glycerine, one ounce of alcohol mixed, then add eight ounces of rose-water.

Another good rule is to rub well in dry oatmeal after every washing, and be particular regarding the quality of soap. Cheap soap and hard water are the unknown enemies of many people, and the cause of rough skin and chapped hands. Castile soap and rain-water will sometimes cure without any other assistance.

Camphor ice is also excellent, and can be applied with but little inconvenience. Borax dissolved and added to the toilet water is also good.

For chapped lips, beeswax dissolved in a small quantity of sweet oil, by heating carefully. Apply the salve two or three times a day, and avoid wetting the lips as much as possible.

To soften the hands : One can have the hands in soap-suds with soft soap without injury to the skin if the hands are dipped in vinegar or lemon juice immediately after. The acids destroy the corrosive effects of the alkali, and make the hands soft and white. Indian meal and vinegar or lemon juice used on hands where roughened by cold or labor will heal and soften them. Rub the hands in this, then wash off thoroughly and rub in glycerine. Those who suffer from chapped hands will find this comforting.

To remove stains, rub a slice of raw potato upon the stains ; or wash the hands in lemon juice or steeped laurel-leaves.

To give a fine color to the nails, the hands and fingers must be well lathered and washed with fine soap ; then the nails must be rubbed with equal parts of cinnebar and emery, followed by oil of bitter almonds. To take white spots from the nails, melt equal parts of pitch and turpentine in a small cup : add to it vinegar and powdered sulphur. Rub this on the nails and the spots will soon disappear.